To Hugh Loebner,
creative to a fault

Creativity Games
for Trainers

Creativity Games for Trainers

A Handbook of Group Activities for
Jumpstarting Workplace Creativity

Robert Epstein

Research Professor
National University
and Director Emeritus
Cambridge Center for Behavioral Studies

Training McGraw-Hill

New York   San Francisco   Washington, D.C.   Auckland   Bogotá
Caracas   Lisbon   London   Madrid   Mexico City   Milan
Montreal   New Delhi   San Juan   Singapore
Sydney   Tokyo   Toronto

Library of Congress Cataloging-in-Publication Data

Epstein, Robert, date.
    Creativity games for trainers : a handbook of group activities for
jumpstarting workplace creativity / Robert Epstein.
        p.   cm.
    Includes bibliographical references.
    ISBN 0-07-021363-1 (pbk.).—ISBN 0-07-912221-3 (looseleaf)
    1. Employees—Training of—Problems, exercises, etc.   2. Creative
ability—Problems, exercises, etc.   3. Creative thinking—Problems,
exercises, etc.   I. Title.
HF5549.5.T7E67   1996
658.3'124—dc20   95-47516
                                                    CIP

McGraw-Hill

A Division of The McGraw·Hill Companies

1 2 3 4 5 6 7 8 9 0 EDW/EDW 9 0 0 9 8 7 6 5 (PBK)
1 2 3 4 5 6 7 8 9 0 EDW/EDW 9 0 0 9 8 7 6 5 (LL)

ISBN 0-07-021363-1 (PBK)
ISBN 0-07-912221-3 (LL)

*The sponsoring editor for this book was Richard Narramore, the editing supervisor was David E. Fogarty,
and the production supervisor was Pamela A. Pelton.*

Printed and bound by Edwards Brothers.

McGraw-Hill books are available at special quantity discounts to use as premiums and sales pro-
motions, or for use in corporate training programs. For more information, please write to the
Director of Special Sales, McGraw-Hill, 11 West 19th Street, New York, NY 10011. Or contact your
local bookstore.

 This book is printed on recycled, acid-free paper containing a
minimum of 50 percent recycled, de-inked fiber.

BRIEF CONTENTS

ANNOTATED CONTENTS

process to function, and they need to master ways to preserve new ideas as they occur.

By enriching the social and physical environments in which people work, we can spur creativity by producing multiple repertoires of behavior.

Participants shift in and out of a team, and the advantages and disadvantages of creating in a team are explored.

INTRODUCTION

Creativity Games is not a book for the fainthearted. It's a blend of serious science (ouch!), strenuous fun (ugh!), and mind-altering challenges (oh no!).

It will make you and your trainees think—about what "creativity" really is, about yourselves as creative people, and about your organization as a creative organization.

It will make your trainees move awkwardly, and look silly, and even play with toys (well, playing with toys isn't so bad, I guess).

It will, I hope, make you and your associates confused—at least temporarily.

It will, shamelessly and unabashedly, make people fail. Uh oh. That's not what you want to hear. You want to *succeed*, right? And you want your colleagues and staff and students to *succeed* as well. Failure is not high on your "to do" list, more likely than not.

But when you take a good, hard, scientific look at the creative process, you come face-to-face with failure—not to mention embarrassment, confusion, frustration, silliness, awkwardness, hesitation, and a host of other phenomena that many people think are bad. These phenomena certainly make us *feel* uncomfortable, even if they may indeed have value.

This book, and the exercises it contains, will, I hope, ease the discomfort, dispel some myths, and greatly increase both the practical and the theoretical understanding of the creative process. Most important, the material in this book will make you and those you work with more creative. For most people, creativity is a vast well of talent that has barely, if ever, been tapped. Fact is, if you're feeling confused, you're in darn good company, and you're probably on the verge of a new idea.

Creativity Games is, I believe, a unique contribution to the ever-swelling flood of creativity books (see the Suggested Readings section at the end of this volume for a sample). It's based on nineteen years of laboratory research which I began as a graduate student at Harvard and which I've continued to pursue as I've shifted from university to university (and from coast to coast!). The research has been reported in *Nature*, *Science*, the *Proceedings of the National Academy of Sciences*, and other scientific journals. In other words, it isn't hype (see Chapter 2).

The research has revealed many of the details of how the creative process works, moment-to-moment in time. For a while, only I and a handful of my scientist colleagues knew about the work. As a matter of course, I eventually started teaching students about it. To facilitate the learning process, I developed and refined various classroom exercises—some of which appear in this volume in modified form.

A few years ago, word began to leak to the "real world" that my colleagues and I knew something special about creativity. I was invited to consult at some major companies, to train teachers, to speak at the National Invention Center, to join the faculty of the Cambridge Forum on Executive Leadership, and so on. I was forced, in effect, to face reality—to build bridges from the esoteric, orderly world of laboratory science to the turbulent, unpredictable, demanding world of the marketplace. The list of exercises grew, and I began to modify them for "real" people—for corporate trainers, for high-school teachers, for parents, and for managers. I even communicated some of this work in a *Reader's Digest* article, which is, I submit, about as real as you can get.

The exercises in this volume reflect my progress *so far*. I emphasize "so far" because the gap between science and application can never be closed entirely. Applications necessarily involve extrapolations, leaps of faith, and complications and complexities that go far afield of basic research. The application of research is a very messy, very tentative, process.

What's more, research itself is never definitive. Research that reaches an endpoint, that yields "all" the answers, is poor—or at least poorly interpreted—research. Careful scientific research on creativity has barely just begun. With luck and perseverance, scientists will continue to shed new light on the creative process for many years to come.

Because the research enterprise is, necessarily, tentative and continuous, I suggested to McGraw-Hill that we make this volume part of the research process itself. To my delight, I've received full cooperation in this effort. Hence, this book is unique in yet another respect: It will allow trainers, managers, and others to collect *data* about creativity, not only for themselves, but for the scientific community (Section 1.1). In other words, those readers who want to participate—by fax, by snail-mail, or by e-mail—can contribute to the larger effort to understand creativity rigorously. In effect, you can help make the *next* edition of this book a far better work.

The structure of this book is simple and straightforward. Chapters 1 and 2 explain how to use the book and review some of the basics of "generativity" theory and research. Chapters 3 through 8 step you through some exercises, tell you how to customize them to suit your needs, and then "debrief" you. Chapter 9 presents some advanced exercises and then discusses the challenge we face when we try to turn raw creativity into useful, marketable products, processes, and services—the things we call "innovations." It's been estimated that it takes many thousands of ideas to produce one marketable product or service. Chapter 9 will suggest a way to streamline the process using methods developed throughout this book. The main focus of the book, however, is on creativity *per se:* methods that will allow us to improve both the quantity and quality of the pool of original ideas from which all good ideas must flow. Without creativity, there can be no innovation.

I've introduced a few technical terms in this volume; the Glossary at the end of the book will, I hope, help to clarify these terms. In the Appendix, I've also included some bare-bones forms that will help trainers to collect data, to get feedback from participants, and to provide feedback to me about the book. For trainers who may want to bring this book home with them, I've also included some brief suggestions for modifying the exercises for home and school use.

This volume takes some risks, ones that are consistent with and suggested by generativity research. I'll give you *some* information and *some* answers and *some* exercises, but I'm also holding back a great deal, and I'm doing so *deliberately*. As I discuss in Chapters 2 and 5, you can't be very creative unless you're frustrated from time to time. If you're spoon fed, you'll just grow fat and lazy. I want you to have some hunger pangs. I want your head to spin. I want you to feel uncertain at times. I want "multiple repertoires" to be battling in your nervous system (Section 2.1). And, of course, I want you to understand *why* this is so important for the creative process. In particular, I have resisted the temptation to provide examples of how particular organizations have applied the principles that are presented in this text. Examples constrain people's thinking and inhibit creativity. Two decades of research have convinced me that people will produce better results if they're given some general principles and then allowed to fend for themselves. As the Talmud says, "Give a man fish, and he will not be hungry. *Teach* a man to fish, and he will *never* be hungry."

I'm grateful to a number of people and organizations for helping bring this volume to life: to Richard Narramore, my editor at McGraw-Hill, for patience and—dare I say it?—creativity; to Shelly Bailey, for editorial assistance; to Dr. Aubrey C. Daniels, Dr. Philip W. Hurst, Dr. Lyle M. Spencer, Jr. (of The Hay Group), and Dr. Edward L. Anderson, Jr. (of the Cambridge Center for Behavioral Studies), for helping me to build bridges; to the Center for Behavioral Epidemiology of the Graduate School of Public Health at San Diego State University, for material support, and especially to Dr. Melbourne F. Hovell, the Center's Director; to the National Science Foundation, the National Institute of Health, Sigma Xi, and Aubrey Daniels and Associates, for material support for the research upon which these exercises are based; to Mr. Norio Nakamoto of the HAL Computer Institute in Osaka, Japan, for encouragement and support; to Dr. Jerry C. Lee, President of National University, for a special appointment and a Presidential Award that helped give me the freedom to work on this volume; and to the many students and research assistants with whom I've had the good fortune to work over the years—for forcing me to pay attention.

Robert Epstein
Cardiff by the Sea, California

Before the beginning of great brilliance,
there must be chaos.
Before a brilliant person begins something great,
he must look foolish to the crowd.

—*I Ching*

Creativity Games
for Trainers

CHAPTER 1

GETTING STARTED

HOW TO USE THIS TEXT

Creativity Games is structured to make life easy—or at least to make creativity easy. Chapters 1 and 2 should be reviewed by all trainers, no matter what application they have in mind. Chapter 2 is especially important, because it gives some basic scientific information, as well as the rationale for the games. Section 2.2 summarizes four practical strategies for promoting creativity, corresponding to the exercises in Chapters 4 through 7 of the book (see below). The Introduction and early chapters also explain how the games and materials in this book can be used to help advance the scientific understanding of creativity.

CHOOSING ACTIVITIES TO MEET
YOUR TRAINING OBJECTIVES

The games themselves are described in Chapters 3 through 9. Each chapter focuses on one overall training objective:

Chapter	Title	Objective
3	*Creativity Games:* Is Everyone Creative?	To convince participants that every one of them, at every level of an organization, has enormous, untapped creative potential.
4	*"Capturing" Games:* Why the Bed, the Bath, and the Bus?	To teach participants basic "capturing" skills—skills that allow us to attend to and preserve the new ideas that never stop running through our heads.
5	*"Challenging" Games:* Can Failure Lead to Success?	To teach participants the important role that failure plays in the creative process, and to help them develop "Controlled Failure Systems" to promote creativity in an organizational setting.
6	*"Broadening" Games:* Can Learning Make Us More Creative?	To teach participants the surprising role that "Diverse Training" plays in creativity and to help them develop creativity-oriented training programs to help promote creativity in their organization.

7	*"Surrounding" Games:* What Should I Put on My Desk?	To teach participants the role that ambiguous, "multiple-controlling" stimuli play in creativity and to help them design the workplace so as to benefit from this phenomenon.
8	*Team Creativity:* Is It Better to Be Alone?	To teach participants the pros and cons of trying to be creative in group settings and to help them design and utilize teams appropriately in the creative process.
9	Keys to Creating Innovative Products, Services, and Processes	To involve participants in advanced exercises that illustrate a number of principles working together, and to help participants put the games into a broader perspective.

Each chapter begins with a brief introductory section—the "Orientation"—which should be carefully reviewed by the trainer before beginning the exercises in that section. If the book is being used in a didactic setting, then all participants should read the introductory section, as well. The Orientation is followed by several games, and they in turn are followed by two special games, the "Design Challenge" and the "Workplace Challenge."

Design Challenge

The Design Challenges have participants design, implement, and conduct a brand new exercise that teaches concepts like the ones they've just learned in previous exercises. The design challenges have very little structure to them—by design, of course. They put trainer and participants into new roles: The participants become trainers and, as the creators of new designs, they also become co-authors of this book. The trainer becomes a participant; trainers can be required by the participants to serve as participants in the new exercises. In my experience, the Design Challenges—although a bit risky—are the most fun, the most interesting, and the most rewarding of the games. They're also the most powerful teaching tools. There's no better way to learn than to teach, and when it comes to creativity, there's no better way to become creative than to promote creativity in others.

Workplace Challenge

The Workplace Challenges give participants an opportunity to apply what they've just learned to their own organizational settings. Participants are asked to devise policies and procedures to beef up creativity in the workplace, to anticipate problems with the new policies and procedures, and to try to solve those problems. This is just an exercise, of course. Not everyone will be able to transfer the results of the exercise to the real world, but at least it's a step. More likely than not, the moment the participants return to their real desks, they'll be swamped with the usual crises—augmented by the fact that they've just returned from a training session and are now farther behind than ever. Follow-up materials included in this volume will allow you to track the success and failure of participants, the ultimate goal being to increase the success rate.

Picking and Choosing Games

It isn't necessary to complete all of the games in each section. Pick and choose to suit your needs, keeping in mind the following provisos: Participants will perform best in a Design Challenge exercise if they've completed all of the preceding exercises in the section. Without this experience, they won't know what to design. Similarly, participants will perform best in a Workplace Challenge exercise if they've completed all of the previous exercises in the section, *including* the Design Challenge. The basic exercises *expose* participants to some new ideas and techniques, but the Design Challenge goes further by asking participants to *utilize* this new material. In other words, the basic exercises facilitate *learning*, whereas the Design Challenge is a step toward *mastery*. Ideally, participants have taken a step toward mastery before trying to apply the new concepts to real situations.

GAME CHAPTERS

Following the introductory section in each chapter, several games are described in detail. For each game, the trainer is given a variety of information for (a) conducting the basic exercise, (b) customizing that exercise, (c) discussing the exercise with the group, (d) collecting data (if applicable), and (e) providing follow-up (if applicable). The material for each game is organized as follows:

> BASICS
> > Objective
> > Brief Description
> > Required Materials and Supplies
> > Optional Materials and Supplies
> > Time Requirement
> PROCEDURE
> > Basic Procedure
> > Customizing the Procedure
> > > *For Small Groups*
> > > *For Large Groups*
> > > *For Non-Business Settings*
> > > *For Schools or Homes*
> > Other Options
> > Data Collection
> FOLLOW-UP
> > Discussion Questions

Debriefing
Long-Term Follow-Up
COMMENTS

Each game chapter also includes figures, charts, and forms that are relevant to the game. These items may be photocopied, cut, pasted, transferred to transparencies, and so on, as needed for each game. Guidelines for using these materials are included in each chapter. Most chapters also include an evaluation form that can be used to improve future training sessions.

TIME REQUIREMENTS

The time required to conduct the exercises varies considerably from one to another; minimum and maximum time estimates are given in each chapter and range from 5 minutes to an hour. A full exploration of each section, with breaks, takes about half a day, and, thus, *a full exploration of this entire book will take three-and-a-half training days, or seven half-day training sessions.* Skipping and condensing here and there, the training time can be reduced to *two full days*.

Design for a Half-Day Workshop

If your goal is simply to expose people—say, upper-level managers—to the techniques, rather than to establish mastery of the material, I'd suggest using six exercises in the following regimen:

The New Science and Technology of Creativity	Draw on material from the Introduction and from Sections 2.1, 2.2, and 2.3.
Is Everyone Creative?	Section 3.2: "Capturing a Daydream" Section 3.3: "Selling a Zork"
The Importance of Capturing	Section 4.2: "The Random Doodles Game"
How Can Failure Help?	Section 5.2: "The Not-for-the-Fainthearted Game"
Creativity and Problem Solving	Section 9.2: "The Keys to Creativity"
Creativity, Innovation, and the Real World	Section 9.4: "The Ultimate Design Challenge" Draw on material from Sections 9.1 and 9.5. Conclude with "The Waiting Game," Section 9.6.

DATA COLLECTION

Forms are included throughout the book that will enable trainers to collect data, should they wish to do so. Not all of the exercises lend themselves to data collection using printed forms; for some, nothing less than a video tape recorder will do (see Section 2.1). Where paper and pencil is adequate, however, trainers are encouraged to collect as much information as time and resources will allow. The data can be used to help trainers or the author to customize and improve the exercises, and they can also be used to advance the scientific understanding of creativity. Ultimately, that will mean more creative people and organizations (see Section 2.4). The forms include information for faxing or e-mailing results to the author for analysis. The Appendix includes forms for the Challenge exercises, as well as forms for collecting feedback about the training workshop or about this text.

ADDITIONAL READINGS

Serious trainers are also serious students, and that means keeping abreast of relevant literature. Some pertinent readings are suggested at the end of the text.

GLOSSARY

A brief Glossary of technical terms is included at the end of the book.

FEEDBACK

The author welcomes constructive feedback about any aspect of this volume, and a form is given at the end of the book to make it easy to get in touch. Revisions of this volume and subsequent books in this series will be responsive to the feedback of readers. If people take the time to comment, they deserve to be heard. The author can be reached by fax at 619-436-4490, by e-mail at repstein@rohan.sdsu.edu, or by telephone at 1-800-BEST-BEHAVIOR (237-8234). Corrections to the book, as well as pertinent notices, will be posted on the author's World Wide Web page: http://rohan.sdsu.edu/faculty/repstein/index.html.

MATERIALS AND SUPPLIES

Each game chapter gives specific recommendations for materials and supplies. Some exercises will require to you obtain strange objects, and I've deliberately given you considerable leeway. Here are some guidelines for obtaining the materials you'll need:

TOY CHEST

If you're a "casual" creativity trainer—that is, if you don't plan to use these games very often—collect the various objects you need, conduct the exercises, and then offer the objects to the participants. This will lighten your load on the way home, and, if you've chosen the objects wisely, it will also increase your popularity. More important, it will help the participants: Souvenirs will help them remember the exercises, and if participants are willing to put some of the objects on display in a work area, the objects may even boost creativity (see Chapters 2 and 7).

If, on the other hand, you plan to repeat these exercises many times with different groups, I strongly recommend that you add a toy chest to your office. This will probably boost your reputation considerably among your colleagues, and it will also save you a lot of time. Some objects are more interesting than others; the toy chest will help you collect and keep track of the most interesting ones. As your collection improves, so will the exercises.

If you need to travel with your materials, as I do, you'll need to select them carefully. Do *not* walk onto an airplane carrying a broom or a baseball bat! (Trust me on that.) I've assembled a traveling kit of materials that's ideal for these exercises and that fits in a single suitcase. I've even got a mop with a telescoping handle. It can be done.

WHERE TO GET THEM

For some of the exercises, all you'll need to do is photocopy the forms or diagrams included in the chapter. You can also modify the forms to suit your needs. Sometimes—especially if you're working with large groups—you will want to create transparencies of these forms and diagrams.

Where props are needed, however, you'll need to be a little more creative (that's what this book is all about, of course). Most of the objects you'll need are common and inexpensive—alphabet blocks, a stool, a key ring, and so on. If you don't already have them at home, you can obtain them easily at any discount store. For some exercises, you'll need to obtain strange or unusual objects (see Figure 3.3.1 for some examples). Although this may sound intimidating, you'll have no trouble at all obtaining them, and they won't cost you a dime. You've got four easy ways to go: Check your garage, your attic, or your basement (that's three, so far); you'll probably find an abundance of unusual items, most of which you don't need and some of which you'd swear you've never even seen before. (Apartment dwellers: Check your storage area or offer to "clean out" a friend's garage.) Your fourth option is the best of all: Ask your *participants* to rummage through *their* garages, attics, and basements. You'll be swamped with the bizarre. When all else fails, *look around the room*. One of the best training sessions I ever gave—one that was great fun and that taught me a great deal—was born of disaster (see Chapters 2 and 5 about the important role that failure plays in creativity). I had grabbed the wrong suitcase, which left me without my props! I asked my limo driver to stop at an all-night drug store on the way to the hotel. That gave me most of what I needed, and the rest came *from the hotel room*.

Again, I need to stress, as I do throughout the book, that you have considerable leeway in selecting and collecting materials. That's the way it should be. It's my job to stimulate creativity; I feel no guilt about starting with the trainer. With considerable control over your materials, it will also be easier for you to customize the exercises so that they have the greatest impact on your trainees.

PROBLEMS AND SUBTLETIES

Murphy's Law is especially pervasive in the world of creativity training, but I've come to realize that snafus help more than they hurt when creativity is on the line. Failure or—"non-reinforcement"—stimulates "the resurgence of multiple repertoires of behavior" (see Chapter 2), and multiple repertoires are the stuff of creativity. It's when ideas compete that new ideas emerge. Hence, when something goes "wrong" in a training session, the outcome can almost always be used to illustrate the concepts you're trying to teach. As you become more seasoned in the use of the exercises in this book, you'll become increasingly comfortable with failure; ideally, you'll also convey that attitude to your participants. In every crisis, there's an opportunity.

That aside, do take care to select appropriate materials. In "The Keys to Creativity" exercise (Section 9.2), for example, the size of the key ring has a big effect on the participant's behavior. If the ring is too large, the problem will be solved quickly in a trivial way; if the ring is too small, the participant may overlook a very promising approach to solving the problem. (Guidelines for handling such situations are given in the chapter).

Creativity training will be more interesting, memorable, and exciting if the unexpected occurs from time to time. But if the unexpected occurs *every* time, your participants will have every right to believe that you've come unprepared. So have fun, but put some effort into selecting your materials and planning your games.

SHARING AND FEEDBACK

Forms throughout this book will allow you to share your experiences with the author. If you've had trouble with some of the recommended materials or you've discovered some superb new ones, please communicate that fact by e-mail or fax.

CHAPTER 2

"GENERATIVITY":
WHY THESE
PARTICULAR GAMES?

THE NEW SCIENCE OF CREATIVITY

All too often, people claim that creativity is mysterious. It isn't—at least, not when you look closely enough. The behavior we call "creative" is actually orderly and predictable when examined carefully in the laboratory. That's good news for those of us who need to promote and enhance creativity in the real world. It means that creativity can be *engineered*—that we can train people to be far more creative than they usually are and that we can change policies and procedures to accelerate creativity in an organization and to direct creativity toward desired ends.

My views on creativity—which, I admit, are not yet commonplace—are based on nearly two decades of laboratory research, work I began as a graduate student in psychology at Harvard University in the 1970s. This volume is not the appropriate place to present this research in detail; however, as a trainer, you may find it helpful to familiarize yourself with some of the basics. This chapter will help you do that.

People tend to respect science, so you may find it easier to persuade and educate if you present the exercises in this book in a scientific framework. You'll find this works especially well when you're working with trainees who are themselves scientists or engineers—with members of a Research and Development department, for example, where both science and creativity are held in high esteem.

Here, then, are some of the basics of Generativity Theory—the formal, empirical, predictive theory of novel behavior upon which the games in this volume are based. As you'll see, the theory has practical applications that will help any organization to boost its creative output substantially.

Generativity Theory

First, a disclaimer. Generativity Theory is best expressed by a series of equations. When instantiated in a computer model, the equations can do some impressive things—like predict a creative performance in an individual, moment-to-moment in time (at least in the laboratory!).

Unfortunately, equations don't sell very well, and words don't do them justice. That said, here are some (imprecise) words about Generativity Theory:

Multiple Repertoires of Behavior

We are all capable of doing many different things in any given situation. If you're alone in your living room, for example, you might turn on the television, change channels, eat a snack, read a book, daydream about your workday, vacuum the rug, do some sit-ups, exercise to an aerobics video, pet your dog, or make a phone call. Depending on the form or "topography" of the behaviors, you can do two or more things at the same time. For example, you can easily pet your dog, eat a snack, and watch television simultaneously. On the other hand, it would be difficult to pet your dog while jumping around to an aerobics video. What's more, on any particular occasion, some of these behaviors will be more likely to occur than others; that is, they will have different "probabilities of occurrence." For example, if you've just come home from a workout at the health club, you're far more likely to watch TV than to do sit-ups.

The items you happen to find in your living room (the "current stimuli") will affect these probabilities. For example, if your dog is in the back yard, you're very unlikely to pet the dog while sitting in the living room (unless, of course, you have *very* long arms). If your VCR is broken—as my living-room VCR happens to be at the moment—you're unlikely to work out to an exercise video in that room. On the other hand, if your dog joins you on the sofa while you're watching television, the likelihood of petting will increase dramatically.

Finally, given the hundreds of things you might do in your living room, it's unlikely, at any given moment, that you'll be doing *only one* of them. We joke that some people can't walk and chew gum at the same time, but that just isn't true. Chances are, you do at least two or three things simultaneously virtually all the time. While doing your sit-ups, for example, you might also think about a heated discussion you had with a colleague at the office, or perhaps you'll fantasize about your upcoming vacation. On the other hand, it's also unlikely that you'll do a hundred things at once, even if it were physically possible to do so. The more things you do simultaneously, the more uncoordinated you become, and the more anxious you feel. If you doubt that, try thinking about your workday while turning in circles, patting the top of your head with one hand, and rubbing your tummy with the other. Now start counting aloud backwards by 7s from 100. As the therapists say, "How does this make you feel?" Not very well, I'd wager.

Here's the general idea so far: In any given situation, *multiple repertoires of behavior are the rule*. The word "behavior" should be interpreted broadly to include just about everything a person can imagine, think, do, or say. Behaviors can occur both sequentially and simultaneously; some are more likely to occur than others; and the situation helps to determine which behaviors occur. As you'll see in a moment, multiple repertoires are the seeds from which new ideas are born; the more seeds, the better, and work environments that stimulate multiple repertoires of behavior will also stimulate more creativity.

Prior History and Individual Differences

To this add the following: You and I will likely do different things in our respective living rooms. In fact, if you paraded a group of people, one by one, into the *same* living room, they'd all do different things there. Why? Well, broadly speaking, there are three reasons, two of which you already know about and the third we'll get to in a moment.

First, we are all unique physically, thanks in large part to the unique set of genes with which we were born. My nervous system is a little different from yours, and that alone will make me behave a little differently than you do in the same situation. Perhaps the dancing set of color images on a television screen is a powerful hypnotic for your nervous system; someone else might barely see it.

Second, we each have a unique "environmental history"—a unique set of experiences, if you will. Among other things, that means that we each bring a unique set of behaviors to any given situation. An artist might draw sketches in her living room; a teacher might grade papers there; an avid reader might curl up with a novel. If the door by which you would normally exit from the living room jams, your method of escape will depend on your previous experience with locked doors. One person will try to shoulder the door open with brute force; another will lift up or push down on the knob; still another will shout for help or dial 911 on the telephone.

Third, generative abilities—the processes that transform old behaviors into new ones—probably differ somewhat from one person to another. The speed with which transformations take place probably differs from body to body, and some of us get frustrated more quickly than others do when multiple behaviors are competing in our nervous systems. We'll explore these issues throughout this book.

So far, here's the gist: *Multiple behaviors are the rule, and we each bring a unique set of behaviors to any given situation.* Our challenge as creativity engineers will be to bring people with just the right training into work environments that accelerate "generative processes." If this seems esoteric, hang in there. We're ultimately going to translate this into specific practices for the organizational setting.

Novelty, Creativity, and Innovation

How do we get from multiple behaviors to the things we really care about, namely, novelty, creativity, and innovation? Each step is straightforward, no matter what you may have heard to the contrary. Let's start with novelty.

Novelty. According to Generativity Theory, novel behavior is the inevitable result of the dynamic competition among repertoires of behavior. In other words, when you're thinking or doing two or more things at the same time, the competing repertoires become *interconnected* to form *new forms* or *new sequences* of behavior. Aha. Given that multiple repertoires are almost always competing in our nervous systems, novel behavior should almost always be occurring. Indeed, that's the case. Behavior is almost always novel, although not necessarily very important.

This is not a very "novel" idea. People have long speculated that new ideas result when old ones come together in some way. The eminent mathematician Henri Poincaré made an important discovery one evening after he had drunk too much coffee. Wrote Poincaré, "Ideas arose in crowds. I felt them collide until pairs interlocked, so to speak, making a stable combination." Einstein attributed his creativity to "combinatory play," and John Dryden, the famous English poet, spoke of "a confus'd mass of Thoughts, tumbling over one another in the Dark." The major difference between Generativity Theory and earlier formulations is that GT is formal and empirical: It can be expressed mathematically; it is substantiated by laboratory research; and it makes specific and testable predictions. In a variety of research with both animals and people, generativity research shows that *the process of interconnection is orderly and predictable.*

Creativity. For the sake of argument, let's assume at this point that we've got a theory that accounts for the fact that people do and think new things much of the time. How do we get from novelty to "creativity"? The key here is *context* or *culture*. "Creative" is a label applied to novel behavior that society (a) recognizes as novel and (b) finds valuable in some way. Sure, you may brush your teeth a little differently each morning, but if that's the best you can do, no one will ever call you "creative." Even a truly amazing achievement will not be dubbed "creative" if someone else has already achieved it. If the Theory of Relativity had already been published before Einstein mailed in his manuscript, the manuscript would have been politely returned, and Albert would have lived out his days as a patent clerk. Try re-inventing the wheel, and see where it gets you.

Bear in mind that groups are fickle in their use of the language of creativity. Recently an art collector in the United States paid more than two million dollars for a painting that was created by naked women dragging their paint-clad bodies across a canvas. In another era the perpetrators of this work of art would have been burned at the stake.

Innovation. For every new product or service that's offered, a great many never see the light of day. In fact, it has been estimated that only *one in twenty thousand* ideas makes it to the marketplace. When creative behavior leads to products, services, or processes that are good enough to make money, we have entered that special realm called "innovation."

To get from creative ideas to innovative ones, two things are necessary: First, you need a large pool of creative ideas; the more, the better. And second, you need efficient and intelligent mechanisms for constantly sifting through the pool and selecting the ideas that are worth pursuing.

The games in this volume focus on creativity per se—that is, on methods for beefing up the creativity pool. These methods in turn can be extended to the problem of designing better selection mechanisms (see Section 9.4).

So *novelty* is a *property* of behavior—one result of "generative" processes in the nervous system which operate continuously in everyone. The language of *creativity* is applied by a group to a small subset of novel behavior—to behavior that has value to the group. And *innovation* refers to a small subset of creative behavior—to behavior that produces products, services, or processes that, for one reason or another, have monetary value.

Generative processes drive this entire sequence. The question is, to what extent can we direct and control these processes to produce more and better outcomes?

The Theory in Words

Here's a brief statement of the theory: Behaviors ("ideas," "thoughts," "actions") are in constant competition in our nervous systems, and a number of simple processes operate simultaneously on all of these behaviors, causing a variety of interactions. One inevitable outcome of this dynamic process is a steady stream of new behaviors. The entire process is orderly and predictable—good news for those of us who care about enhancing creativity and innovation. *By changing the number and type of behaviors that compete, we can accelerate the creative flow and direct it in desired ways* (more to follow in Section 2.2). That's what we do in the laboratory, and when we teach people about creativity, we give them the tools they need to enhance and direct the creative process in the real world.

To simplify matters even further, new ideas emerge as old ideas compete with each other, and the process by which that happens is orderly. In the workplace, this means that we accelerate and direct the creative process: We can accelerate the creativity machine and even make it run down certain paths. If you want your employees to design better widgets, there are specific ways in which you can train them, modify their work environment, and change your procedures to do just that.

For more details about Generativity Theory and research, you may want to consult some of the references listed in the Suggested Readings section at the end of this volume. Figures 2.1.1 to 2.1.3 can be used to help introduce your trainees to some of the basics of GT.

Figure 2.1.1. *New Ideas* = *f* (*Old Ideas*).

OLD IDEAS

NEW IDEAS

Figure 2.1.2. *Generativity Theory Basics.*

GENERATIVITY BASICS

_____

COMPETING BEHAVIORS PRODUCE NEW ONES

THE COMBINATORIAL PROCESS IS ORDERLY AND PREDICTABLE

BY INFLUENCING THE TYPE AND NUMBER OF COMPETING BEHAVIORS, WE CAN ACCELERATE THE CREATIVE PROCESS AND DIRECT IT TOWARD USEFUL ENDS

Figure 2.1.3. Implications.

SOME IMPLICATIONS
OF GENERATIVITY THEORY

- ## EVERYONE IS CREATIVE

- ## "CREATIVE" PEOPLE HAVE SPECIAL SKILLS

- ## ANYONE CAN LEARN SUCH SKILLS

FOUR STRATEGIES FOR ENHANCING CREATIVITY

We've learned that a competition among different behaviors is essential to the creative process. How can we facilitate that competition, and how can we direct the process to achieve desired goals? In an organizational setting, how can we improve training, change the work environment, and modify policies and procedures to boost creativity?

Generativity Theory suggests four strategies for enhancing and directing creativity. I'll explain these briefly below, along with the scientific rationale for each strategy. The games in Chapters 4 through 7 of the book help teach each of these strategies, and the Workplace Challenges will encourage participants to devise methods for applying these strategies to their particular work situations. You'll find additional information about the strategies in both the Orientation and Debriefing sections in each chapter.

STRATEGIES

The word "strategy" can mean different things in different contexts. In this volume it means a *skill set*—in other words, a set of skills that serve roughly the same function. A marketing strategy is a plan that directs a variety of actions toward one goal: to create an environment for selling a particular product or service. Without a strategy, one can still achieve one's goal, but one will tend to act aimlessly and inefficiently.

There are many possible ways to enhance and direct creative efforts; the four general strategies described here will allow you to use resources wisely and efficiently to manage creativity in an organization. Each strategy derives from specific principles of generativity. The four strategies are:

- **Capturing**

- **Challenging**

- **Broadening**

- **Surrounding**

CAPTURING

Generative mechanisms never stop operating—even while we're asleep. That means that in some sense we're always "creative," or at least we're always thinking new things. As children, we paid close attention to this endless generative flow. We observed it, talked about, and acted on it regularly. Unfortunately, in grade school most of us were persuaded to ignore the extraordinary idea factory in our heads. Your first task as a trainer will be to convince your trainees—or at least to remind them—that this idea factory still exists. The exercises in Chapter 3 will help you begin that task.

Your next task is every bit as important: It's to teach your trainees some basic *capturing skills*—skills that will allow them to attend to and preserve the new ideas that keep coursing through their heads. That's what Chapter 4 is all about.

All of the people whom, as a culture, we label "creative"—artists, inventors, writers, composers, great chefs, and so on—have superb capturing skills. Capturing is a strategy in the sense that it encompasses hundreds of possible skills, practices, and procedures. Your task will be to help your students design capturing skills that are appropriate to their own lives and work settings.

In organizational settings, there are innumerable ways to promote good capturing. Sometimes, you just need the right supplies. We've all heard of suggestion boxes, but what about Idea Pads, Idea Folders, and Idea Boxes? Because people are often reluctant to share their ideas, one of the most powerful ways to promote capturing is through Anonymous Suggestions Systems—suggestion systems that allow people to submit their ideas anonymously but then to claim them later. More about this in Chapter 4.

CHALLENGING

We've seen that new ideas occur when old ones compete. The more behaviors there are competing, the more likely it is that new ideas will arise. So mechanisms that get *more* behaviors going simultaneously have special value in accelerating creativity.

One of the most powerful mechanisms we know about for getting many behaviors to clash and crash against each other is plain-old, vanilla-flavored *failure*. We induce failure in a laboratory setting with a procedure called "extinction," which is, simply, the withholding of reinforcers. Extinction (or "failure," if you prefer) produces a number of effects: It gets people (and animals) upset ("emotional effects"). It makes us abandon our fruitless efforts (a "deceleration of the target behavior"). It makes us push and pull harder, at least for a while ("variations in magnitude and force of responding").

Most important for creativity, extinction produces a *"resurgence* of previously reinforced behavior." That is, when we're failing, we try just about everything we've every done before to help us get out of our predicament.

Hmmm. Let's think about this. You're locked in the living room. The door is jammed. What happens?

Well, you get upset. You push and pull harder. The door still won't give, so you eventually stop pushing. And then what?

That depends on your particular environmental history. Perhaps you shout for help. Or remove the pins from the door hinges. Or break down the door with a chair. Or climb out a window. Or cry out for your mom. In other words, you do whatever you have done in the past that has gotten you through a locked door. As Poincaré said, behaviors "arise in crowds"—especially, it seems, when you're failing.

Let's say all of these attempts to exit have failed, so you're still stuck in the room. What happens next?

The answer, of course, is that the many ideas that are colliding in your head start to come together in new ways. In other words, you start to get creative.

Chapter 5 in this text will help you show your trainees how extremely valuable failure is to the creative process. More important, it will allow the participants to develop "controlled failure systems"—procedures that take advantage of the power of failure without undermining self-esteem. You want your people to have more creativity, not more anxiety attacks.

BROADENING

Competing repertoires have to come from somewhere. In other words, there need to be some old behaviors before we can get new ones. Here's where training and education can made a critical difference. By providing the right sorts of education, we can affect the creative process in two important ways:

First, we can increase the *number* of behaviors that might turn up in a tough situation. James Bond and Harry Houdini would have, at their fingertips, many ways of escaping our locked living room—no creativity needed. The more training we provide that's relevant to the problem area, the more quickly solutions will arise.

Second, we can be selective about the *type* of training we provide. The more *diverse* the training, the wilder and more interesting the solutions. Edwin Land's diverse background in chemistry and optics allowed him, rather suddenly, to envision the instant-photography process. Diverse training is generally your best bet when you're after profound shifts. On the other hand, if you have specific and fairly routine problems to solve in your company, you'll want to provide as much *relevant* training as possible. This is one of the most powerful tools we have for *directing* the creative process toward certain specific ends. You'll find more about broadening, along with some illustrative exercises, in Chapter 6.

SURROUNDING

To get the generativity gears going rapidly, we need to get more repertoires competing. One way to do this is by taking advantage of the resurgence phenomenon: If you make people fail (preferably, in a controlled and non-threatening way), many behaviors will begin to compete, and new behaviors will result. The second way to get multiple behaviors going is jazzing up the environment—by presenting "multiple controlling stimuli."

Say you're approaching a stoplight that isn't working very well. Specifically, the red and green lights are both illuminated. (This actually happened to me once. Am I the only one?) What happens? Well, first of all, you feel confused—a sure sign that behaviors are starting to compete. Second, your right foot does a strange little dance: It shifts back and forth from the accelerator pedal to the brake pedal, briefly hovering in between. In other words, given the stimuli that control both stopping and going, you try to *stop* and *go* at the same time. Multiple controlling stimuli produce multiple behaviors.

By controlling and changing the stimuli that surround us as we work and play, we can have a profound effect on our creativity. What's more, by manipulating the type and number of stimuli that surround us, we can direct the creative process toward useful ends.

In an office environment, this can mean some pretty straightforward practices: wall charts, new desk arrangements, new meeting combinations, and so on. Chapter 7 will help participants design particular methods of surrounding that suit their work environments and goals.

Figure 2.2.1 can be used to introduce or to recap the discussion in this section.

Figure 2.2.1. Four Strategies.

FOUR STRATEGIES
FOR
ENHANCING CREATIVITY

- **CAPTURING**

- **CHALLENGING**

- **BROADENING**

- **SURROUNDING**

DISPELLING THE MYTHS

Myths about creativity abound, but no matter how many times they're repeated, they're myths, nonetheless. (I've heard that repetition is the mother of wisdom, but that shouldn't apply when we're repeating nonsense.) As a trainer, you may want to talk about some of the common myths and then promise, through the games, to dispel them.

MYTH: CREATIVITY IS RARE

Generativity research demonstrates fairly definitively that the mechanisms that underlie creativity are universal. Everyone has them. We couldn't function without them. Of course, even with generative mechanisms operating nonstop, that doesn't mean we all are capable of producing *valuable* new things that society will call "creative." Or does it?

Let's think about this. If new ideas are popping into everyone's head virtually all the time—and if indeed we know how to accelerate and direct this process—why *can't* everyone be creative? Why can't we all be Dalis and Beethovens and Lands and Keseys and Shakespeares?

As far as I know, *we can,* and this is not hype. (I promised no hype in this book, remember?)

If we all have enormous creative potential, where the heck is it, you ask? Well, creativity *seems* rare for two reasons, both fairly simple: First, as noted in the previous chapter, very few of us have any capturing skills to speak of. Indeed, when we enter grade school, we are taught, forcefully, to *stop* paying attention to the creative flow.

Some of us discover it again later in life. Take me, for example. Like most people, I love music, and, like most people, I sing strange tunes in the shower, make up my own words to other people's songs, and so on. A few years ago—inspired by one of my own seminars!—I finally took the hint. I started composing for real. All I needed to get going was some relevant capturing skills: Composers use a special notation to help them record their ideas. No sweat. I learned the notation, started carrying a tape recorder everywhere I went, and invested in some helpful software. Some of my compositions have been performed, and I feel that I have hardly begun to explore this new side of me.

I've noticed that my younger son hums and sings strange songs throughout the day. Will society shut him down as well? Will he have to wait until middle age to rediscover this ability?

There is a second reason why so few of us are labeled "creative." The label is reserved for products that are seen as *valuable* at the moment. Once we start paying attention to the creative flow and preserving pieces of it, how do we guarantee value?

This is easier than you think. You've seen professional photographers taking pictures of models on television. How many pictures do they take for every one they actually use? *Hundreds.* Professional creators generate a great deal of output and then *discard the garbage.*

It's that simple, and, needless to say, the more novel output you generate, the more you'll have that's worth preserving.

Years ago I attended the opening of the Helga exhibit at a museum in Boston—an exhibit of hundreds of heretofore unknown drawings and paintings by Andrew Wyeth. Because of Wyeth's fame, the collection was more or less unexpurgated; even the preliminary sketches were shown. (I learned later from a neighbor of his that people frequently search his garbage pails looking for scraps of drawings; even crumpled, smelly scraps have value when you're famous enough.) I was greatly encouraged by what I saw: Most of the drawings were just plain awful—so crude and simple and ordinary that any of us could have drawn them. If these are the ones he's allowing the public to see, I thought, imagine the junk he's given to the garbage-pickers!

The bottom line: *Everyone is creative. No exceptions.* Some people just need to be told, and the floodgates open. Others will need you to step them through some exercises (Chapter 3). Others will need to sharpen various skills (Chapters 4 through 7).

MYTH: ONLY ARTISTS HAVE IT

I'll be brief here, because by now you get the picture (no pun intended). Artists carry sketchpads. Inventors carry notebooks. Composers carry tape recorders or composition books. Writers jot ideas down on napkins. The people we call "creative" have simple skills that anyone can learn. Period.

MYTH: ONLY HIGH IQ'S HAVE IT

This one is tricky. Various studies over the years have identified a correlation between creativity and intelligence. Studies of this sort are "correlational," and such studies are necessarily subject to many different interpretations. It is certainly not the case that one *must* have a high IQ in order to be creative; as I noted before, the generative apparatus is universal. The correlation may exist simply because the high-IQ types take the trouble to learn capturing skills before the rest of us do, or perhaps they're just more ambitious. They may also pay closer attention to what the culture happens to value at the moment. Perhaps they're just better at marketing their ideas. In any case, they don't have any special rights to the creative process. As far as I can tell, everyone has equal creative potential.

MYTH: YOU NEED TO HIRE IT

As a true world economy has taken shape in recent years, so has competition become more intense in many industries. With increased competition, the need for creativity has also grown. Needless to say, wherever a need exists, people turn up who try to profit from it. Some of the early pioneers in creativity training, like Edward deBono, have now been joined by hundreds of consultants, centers, and institutes—the modern creativity industry. Some companies even keep "creative" people on retainers, so that they won't go to the competitors.

There's a place for hired guns who help you educate people about the creative process and who help you implement policies and procedures to enhance and direct creativity. But creativity itself does not need to be hired. The untapped creative potential in your own organization should keep you busy for at least the next hundred years.

There is an exception, however. To tackle certain problems, people have to have the right backgrounds. Broadening (see Section 2.2) takes some time. If you're in a rush, you may need to hire people who can bring the right "repertoires" to the task at hand.

MYTH: IT'S IN YOUR RIGHT BRAIN

This one is a hoax, outright—at least the way it's perpetuated in the pop culture. The brain-hemisphere distinction is based largely on observations of a very small number of "split-brain" patients—roughly forty, in all. The observations, first reported in the 1960s, suggested that the two halves of the brain serve radically different functions. In the 1980s a number of researchers concluded that the original reports had been misinterpreted. The problem is that the split brains—brains that surgeons had deliberately cut in two—were highly abnormal to begin with (that's why the surgery was required), and they were even more abnormal afterwards. The generalizations that early researchers made about the two halves of the brain have not stood the test of time.

Even more important, *virtually no one has a split brain!* The two halves of the brain are connected by a huge structure called the *corpus callosum*, and they are also in touch with each other through the sense organs. The two hemispheres do not function independently in people with intact brains. For all practical purposes, hemisphere differences—to the extent that they exist at all—are minuscule.

For further details, you might want to consult Robert Efron's 1990 book, *The Decline and Fall of Hemispheric Specialization*, or any number of reviews in the business literature by Terence Hines and others.

MYTH: IT'S MYSTERIOUS

To most people, computers are mysterious. They are, to be sure, exceedingly complex devices. What's more, they operate at very high speeds, typically performing millions of operations each second. That's a bit overwhelming—*except to the people who designed the hardware and wrote the programs*.

Creativity, too, involves a great many operations occurring at a relatively high speed, and it, too, is the product of extremely sophisticated hardware (the brain!). But that does not mean that it cannot be understood.

I apologize for that double negative, but I offer no apologies for demystifying creativity. When you look very closely at a creative performance—for example, by examining children's behavior frame by frame on a video tape—you see enormous order. Moreover, when you simulate a creative performance on a computer—by subjecting the probabilities of many different behaviors to many different processes simultaneously—you can actually predict what people do.

In our everyday routine, computers will always seem mysterious, because the hardware is so complex and the speeds are so daunting. Similarly, in our everyday routine, creativity will always seem mysterious. We'll always feel confused and frustrated when ideas are colliding; we'll always be impressed when someone else has a great idea. But the creative process is no less orderly.

Figure 2.3.1 lists some of the common myths about creativity.

Figure 2.3.1. *Myths.*

MYTHS ABOUT CREATIVITY

- IT'S RARE

- ONLY ARTISTS HAVE IT

- ONLY HIGH IQ'S HAVE IT

- YOU NEED TO HIRE IT

- IT'S IN YOUR RIGHT BRAIN

- IT'S MYSTERIOUS

GAMES THAT TEACH

The games in this text were designed to serve several functions. As a trainer, you can focus on the functions that best suit your needs. Here are the most important functions, along with more of the scientific rationale:

DECREASE INHIBITIONS

Virtually all of the games in this book will help "loosen people up." In the context of Generativity Theory, this means simply that the trainer will instruct people to attend to, preserve, and act on their creative ideas. The trainer will also provide challenges and various objects and materials to enhance and direct the creative flow.

In most organizational settings, people would still be uptight, even with all this prompting. In a training session on creativity, however, most everyone loosens up and gets "creative." Why? Because in a training session the usual consequences for demonstrating one's creativity—ridicule, scorn, psychiatric referrals, and so on—are absent. Since elementary school, it's been those ugly consequences that have held most of us back. Remove the aversive consequences, and the creativity gets expressed.

One of the greatest challenges to an organization is to implement policies and procedures that will allow creativity to flourish on a regular basis. The Workplace Challenges throughout this volume will give participants a framework for designing the necessary changes.

ENCOURAGE CREATIVE BEHAVIOR

The games in this volume are also intended to help generate some wild, raucous, knee-slapping creativity—some new behavior that has no immediate use but that will help convince people that they are creative. For some participants, this experience alone may have an important impact; it may even transfer to the work setting. A few weeks after a seminar I gave in Georgia, I received a copy of a six-page sermon that had recently been delivered in a large Catholic church in the Chicago area. The author had translated some of the exercises we had done into a proposal for introducing more creativity into the workings of the church. (What happened to him after this, I can only imagine.) Some people turn to poetry; one poem I received, written by an executive at a gas company in the midwest, was about the creative process itself. Anything can happen when you open the floodgates of creativity, and at least a portion of what is generated is bound to have some value.

GENERATE PRACTICAL IDEAS

Generativity Theory also suggests that creativity can be directed toward useful ends, and some of the games in the volume will help to demonstrate the possibilities. The Workplace Challenges direct the creative process mainly through the instructions that are given to the participants, but GT suggests a number of ways to channel the creative process toward useful outcomes:

- **Instructions** can help channel the process, but other methods will prove to be more powerful in the long run. The "seven hats" method recommended by deBono is an example of an instruction-driven method for channeling the creative process. All instructions do, really, is give people criteria for *selecting* which ideas to report to the team. In fact, they experience many more than they report.

- The creative process can also be directed by careful selection of the **materials, supplies, equipment, and resources** on hand. Current stimuli help to determine *which* repertoires will compete, and that determines which new ideas will turn up. Diverse materials can help to produce more interesting ideas.

- The type of **training** you provide will also make a difference. You're unlikely to get relevant solutions if relevant repertoires are not available.

CONVEY KNOWLEDGE ABOUT THE CREATIVE PROCESS

Perhaps the most important function of the games in this volume is to teach participants about the creative process itself. I've always been a strong believer in that old Talmudic dictum about *teaching* people to fish. The games teach and demonstrate how the creative process works. If participants go back to their workplaces or homes knowing something about "resurgence," "controlled failure systems," "multiple controlling stimuli," and so on, they will be more effective *creators* of their own creativity techniques—in fact, of their own destinies.

These games were designed to loosen people up, to let people be creative in fun ways, and, most important of all, to teach. It is through this last function that they can have their greatest impact.

That said, let the games begin.

CHAPTER 3

CREATIVITY GAMES:
IS EVERYONE CREATIVE?

CREATIVITY: **ORIENTATION**

The generative mechanisms that underlie creativity operate all the time in everyone. In a sense, we all have equal creative potential (see Chapter 2 for further details). Unfortunately, most of us have been trained since our first days in school to ignore the flow of new ideas that constantly surges through our brains. But the flow is there, nonetheless.

The exercises in the chapters that follow will help you show people, quickly and clearly, that the creative flow they left behind at age six is still going strong. In the first exercise, called "Capturing a Daydream," participants are asked simply to relax and let their minds wander. Almost everyone wanders out of the room; many people wander to remote corners of the world; and some people wander to worlds unknown. By taking people on this simple journey, you help them to take the first step toward enhanced creativity: you help them *pay attention* to the flow of novel ideas, images, and perceptions from which all creativity emerges.

In the second exercise, "Selling a Zork," participants are asked to sell some strange objects to the group. People can usually do this easily, even though they've never seen the objects before and even though they have no idea what functions the objects could possibly serve. This exercise involves more *active* and *practical* creativity than the previous one. Guidelines for selecting the objects (or for using the drawings provided in the book) are included in the chapter.

The third exercise, "The *Srtcdjgjklered* Game," is great fun, and it can be conducted in a number of different ways, depending on the time you have available (see that section for guidelines). In one variation, participants tell stories in which they have to transform nonsense words into parts of the story at various points.

To introduce these exercises, you may want to use some of the material from Chapter 2 of this book. If appropriate, introduce Generativity Theory, or simply assert that recent research shows definitively that everyone is creative. Ask how many people believe that, and ask them why they do or don't believe it.

Because the exercises are fun and lecturing isn't, you should keep your introductory material short. You may even want to start your session with the "Daydream" exercise, after which you can begin to make some general comments about creativity, distribute your materials, and state your goals for the training session.

EXERCISE:
"CAPTURING A DAYDREAM"

BASICS

Objective

To convince people that they are creative.

Brief Description

The trainer asks the group to daydream for a few minutes and then asks some individuals to relate to the group the contents of their daydreams. Almost always, a number of people in the room will report bizarre thoughts and images that have taken them far outside the immediate environment or, in some cases, far outside reality.

Required Materials and Supplies

No special materials or supplies are required.

Optional Materials and Supplies

Writing materials for each participant. If data will be collected for later use, Form 3.2.1 can be used in place of plain paper.

Time Requirement

Minimum: 10 minutes. Maximum: 30 minutes.

PROCEDURE

Basic Procedure

Everyone should be seated. Trainer (using language that's comfortable and appropriate): "We're going to play a game now called 'Capturing a Daydream.' Please put down your pencils and get into a relaxed sitting position. In just a minute, I'm going to ask you to do something that you were taught not to do as children. Try to put your inhibitions aside and follow along. I'll do the exercise with you.

"First, we're going to close our eyes and take a deep breath together, just to help us relax. Then, for about five minutes, all you need to do is let your mind wander freely—to any place, any time, any world, any reality. You may see or hear or smell or feel strange things. Don't worry about it. Just keep going. Usually, when people daydream, they don't pay much attention to what they're experiencing. For this exercise, I *do* want you to pay attention. So let your minds wander freely, but keep an eye on what's happening. After five minutes have passed, I'll ask you to open your eyes and then I'll ask some of you to share your daydream with the group. If you need to censor your daydream or you don't want to share it, that's quite alright. But still try to remember it for your own benefit. Any questions?

"Okay, let's begin. Let's close our eyes. Now, together, let's take a deep breath in and then let it out very slowly, blowing away all of the tension in our bodies as we breathe out.... Now, let your minds wander freely, and I'll get back to you in a few minutes...."

After some time has passed, the trainer asks participants to open their eyes and then asks for volunteers to report on what they experienced. This should proceed in two phases:

1) Trainer: "Did anyone leave this room?" A number of people will raise their hands, and the trainer should ask several of them to report on where they went and what they experience there, without offering any analysis.

2) Trainer: "Did anyone experience anything that couldn't possibly be real—for example, seeing the Eiffel Tower upside down, or hearing strange noises or seeing bizarre images, or perhaps flying without an airplane?" A smaller number of people will raise their hands, and, again, the trainer should ask them to report their experiences as well as they can.

Customizing the Procedure

For Small Groups. If there is sufficient time, everyone in a small group should be given a chance to talk about his or her daydream—even if it was mundane. Some people will have trouble "loosening up" after a single experience of this sort. If time allows, the exercise should be repeated, both to allow more people to have a bizarre daydream and to show dramatically an individual's daydreams will *differ* from one try to the next.

For Large Groups. This exercise can be done successfully in large auditoriums with very large audiences. If time is limited, five or six people can usually be called on to share some aspect of their daydream. A remote microphone is helpful in very large rooms.

For Non-Business Settings. This exercise is ideal for a wide range of settings. It can even be used in hospital settings with impaired groups, with the instructions modified appropriately.

For Schools or Homes. With children, it may be inappropriate for the trainer to participate in the exercise. Standing in front of a group of children with your eyes closed can lead to trouble. Because children daydream easily, the dream time can also be shortened considerably. Even a minute may be adequate.

Other Options

If appropriate, as soon as you have had the participants open their eyes, have them jot something down about what they just experienced. Daydreams, like night dreams, disappear quickly from memory. Taking notes helps keeps the memory fresh.

Data Collection

Depending on your needs, you can have participants record some notes about their daydreams on blank sheets of paper (names are not needed) or on Form 3.2.1. In either case, you may find it helpful to collect the notes and then to display some of them on a bulletin board in a common area, or on a computer bulletin board in your organization—especially the examples that might be helpful to your organization. It's important to begin to advertise the fact that "all of us here are creative" and to convince people that creativity is valued in your organization.

FOLLOW-UP

Discussion Questions

1) Did our daydreams take any of us outside of this environment? How far? Who went where?

2) Did our daydreams take any of us outside of reality? Give some examples.

3) Did any of us have difficulty with this exercise? If so, why? Could the present conditions be the problem? Under what conditions might we be able to perform better than we did here?

4) Were any of you surprised by how far your daydreams took you? Why were you surprised?

5) Do you think daydreaming might have any practical value? How so?

6) What is a daydream? Where does the material come from?

7) What does this exercise teach us?

Debriefing

The trainer should try to relate the outcome of the exercise to people's preconceptions about creativity. Key points: (a) Under ideal conditions, every one of us will have highly imaginative daydreams. (b) The daydream is a simple tool that shows us the enormous creative potential we all have. (c) Many of the images people saw here today are every bit as interesting and original and imaginative as the images we see in the greatest surrealist paintings. (Showing a print of Dali's famous "Time Warp" painting or another powerful painting of this sort can drive the point home for many participants.) (d) As other exercises will show even more dramatically, "regular" people may differ from "creative" people only in their willingness to *pay attention* to an internal creative flow and to *record* or *"capture"* new and interesting ideas that occur to them (see the remainder of this section and all of Chapter 4).

Long-Term Follow-Up

No long-term follow-up is required for this exercise.

COMMENTS

This is a simple exercise that almost always has a dramatic impact. It reminds people of something they have been dimly aware of most of their lives: that we all have imaginations as rich as Salvador Dali's but that we seldom pay attention to what our imaginations generate. I've had good results with this exercise with audiences worldwide—even in Japan, where people tend to be inhibited in group settings. One Japanese worker reported, "I saw myself sitting on top of the office building next door, eating a sandwich, and watching this building slowly collapse as if it were being crushed by a giant's foot."

Participant's Notes and Evaluation
Exercise: "Capturing a Daydream"

Please recount your daydream:

"Capturing a Daydream" (Continued)

Participant's name and contact information (optional):

_____

_____

_____

_____

Organization:

_____

_____

Position:

_____

_____

Date:

_____

_____

Trainer:

_____

_____

Value of the exercise:

LOW ☐ ☐ ☐ ☐ ☐ HIGH

Suggestions for improving the exercise:

_____

_____

_____

_____

_____

To share data or comments with the author, fax this form to 619-436-4490.

*From **Creativity Games for Trainers**, by Dr. Robert Epstein. E-mail address: repstein@rohan.sdsu.edu.*

EXERCISE: "SELLING A ZORK"

BASICS

Objective

To convince people that they are creative, not just as passive observers of a daydream, but as speakers, performers, and persuaders.

Brief Description

Participants are asked to sell a strange object to the group.

Materials and Supplies

The sky is the limit. The "Zork" can be almost anything, as long as it's unusual. It should *not* be an object that normally appears in the work setting, and it *must not* be a product that's normally manufactured or sold by the organization. It can be of almost any size, and it may be advantageous to use an object that's so small that the audience can barely see it; that puts even more pressure on the salesperson to be inventive. The best place to find suitable objects? Your basement or attic or garage. You'll be amazed at the number of items in these obscure locations which (a) couldn't possibly be yours, and (b) you cannot identify.

If you'd rather not use an object, feel free to enlarge copies of any of the objects pictured in Figure 3.3.1.

You should have at least three objects ready for each of the volunteer salespeople in the exercise. The objects or drawings should be placed out of sight in the front of the room before the exercise begins.

Time Requirement

Minimum: 15 minutes. Maximum: 1 hour.

PROCEDURE

Basic Procedure

Trainer (modify as appropriate): "The weird and random thoughts and images that run through our heads sometimes certainly seem creative, but does that mean that we can also *act* creatively? In this next exercise, called 'Selling a Zork,' we'll find out. First, I'll need three volunteers....

"All of the volunteers may stay in the room during the exercise, but I'll need them to come to the front of the room one at a time. Will my first volunteer come to the front of the room and face the audience?

"Now I'm going to show you three objects, one at a time, by holding them up behind our volunteer's back, so that our volunteer can't see them.... Here is Object 1.... Here is Object 2.... And here is Object 3....

"In just a moment, I'm going to ask our volunteer to sell you one of these objects. You, the members of the audience, get to choose which one it will be. All those for Object 1? For Object 2? For Object 3?

"Okay. Volunteer, *this* is a 'Zork.' You have three minutes in which to sell it to this audience. The asking price is $250,000."

The trainer should repeat this procedure with each volunteer, asking for even more money for each new Zork. With a suitable selection of objects, everyone should have great fun.

Customizing the Procedure

For Small Groups. In small a group, everyone can play the salesperson role. If necessary, the main group can be broken up into smaller groups to speed things up. The larger the number of small groups, the more Zorks you'll need.

For Large Groups. In a large group, you may want to stick with a small number of volunteers who give their presentation to the entire audience.

For Non-Business Settings. In any setting, the objects should be as strange as possible.

For Schools or Homes. This is a great exercise for kids of any age. If the participants are timid, or unsure about what the task is, the trainer or teacher might start the exercise by having the children select a Zork for the trainer to sell.

Other Options

Any of the parameters can be altered to suit the situation: the number of volunteers, the presentation time for each volunteer, and the selection of Zorks.

Data Collection

Form 3.3.1 or an equivalent can be used to facilitate data collection.

FOLLOW-UP

Discussion Questions

1) What kinds of objects or drawings could be used as Zorks in this exercise? Is there any limit?

2) Even though a Zork can be almost anything—real or imaginary—is there anyone here today who believes they could *not* sell a Zork to the group? If so, please explain. Could we change the exercise in some way to make it easier for you to sell a Zork?

3) How is it that we're able to sell Zorks, even though we've never seen them before?

4) Is Zork-selling "creative"? Why or why not?

5) If you can sell a Zork, what else might you able to do that you're not doing now?

6) How, if at all, might Zork-selling be relevant to your organization?

Debriefing

Trainer: "In our day-to-day routine, most of us would have trouble writing a ten-word jingle for our favorite breakfast cereal. Yet—as we've seen today—most of us can easily sell a $250,000 Zork, even though (a) we've never seen it before, and (b) it looks ridiculous. It seems that in the right setting—*and given the appropriate permission*—we can 'switch on' a very high degree of creativity. Let's see if we take this even further in the next exercise."

Long-Term Follow-Up

This exercise does not require long-term follow-up, but, as in other exercises, the trainer should make a record of remarkable results (Form 3.3.1 might be helpful) and, if possible, post them prominently for others in the organization to see. The more we grant "permission" for people to be creative, the better.

COMMENTS

The more provocative and interesting the selection of Zorks, the more successful this exercise will be. Select your pool of Zorks to suit the crowd. Allow the audience to make the final selection to keep enthusiasm high.

Figure 3.3.1. *Sample Zorks.*

Participant's Notes and Evaluation
Exercise: "Selling a Zork"

Please sketch a Zork:

In what ways might the salesperson's presentation be considered "creative"?

Could you sell this Zork?   Yes ☐   No ☐   How?

To share data or comments with the
author, fax this form to 619-436-4490.

From Creativity Games for Trainers, by Dr. Robert
Epstein. E-mail address: repstein@rohan.sdsu.edu.

"Selling a Zork" (Continued)

Participant's name and contact information (optional):

_____

_____

_____

_____

Organization:

_____

_____

Position:

_____

_____

Date:

_____

_____

Trainer:

_____

_____

Value of the exercise:

LOW　　☐　　　☐　　　☐　　　☐　　　☐　　HIGH

Suggestions for improving the exercise:

_____

_____

_____

_____

_____

EXERCISE: "THE *SRTCDJGJKLERED* GAME"

BASICS

Objective

To loosen people up, to have some fun, and to provide further evidence that everyone is creative—this time, by using ambiguous stimuli to control speech.

Brief Description

Participants are asked to tell a story using nonsensical terms that are difficult to pronounce.

Required Materials and Supplies

This exercise can be done in a number of different ways to suit the occasion (see below). For the basic exercise, trainers will need (a) slips of paper containing sentences that tell a simple story, (b) slips of paper or cards containing nonsense words, and (c) a handout for the group containing all of the nonsense words. In place of a handout, the words can be projected on a screen using an overhead projector. Figures 3.4.1 and 3.4.2 can be used to create these materials.

Optional Materials and Supplies

Trainers are free to create their own stories and their own nonsense words. The exercise can also be expanded to allow the participants themselves to create these materials (see below for suggestions).

Time Requirement for the Basic Exercise

Minimum: 5 minutes. Maximum: 15 minutes.

PROCEDURE

Basic Procedure

Trainer (modify as appropriate): "This next exercise is fun, brief, and distinctive. What distinguishes it from most exercises is its name, which is: 'The *Srtcdjgjklered* Game.' I'll need five volunteers to come to the front of the room. You're going to be our storytellers in this game."

The trainer recruits the storytellers and gives each of them (a) a slip of paper containing part of the story and (b) a slip of paper containing a nonsense word. The trainer then distributes the list of nonsense words (but not the story!) to the entire group, or displays the list of nonsense words (but not the story!) on a screen using an overhead projector or computer display.

Trainer: "Okay, storytellers. Your task now is to tell us the story I've given you, called 'How Pat Got Promoted from a Mail-Room Job to the Presidency of the Company.' Going from left to right down our row of storytellers, I'd like each of you to tell us a piece of the story. Where material is missing, use the nonsense words I've provided to fill in as best you can. Any questions?"

If time allows, have the storytellers trade slips and retell the story.

Customizing the Procedure

For Small Groups. By changing the story or creating a new one, you can have everyone tell part of the story. People should be seated around a table or in a circle to facilitate interaction.

For Large Groups. Selecting a small number of storytellers to speak to the group should work well. If time allows, you can have another group of storytellers tell a second story, and so on.

For Business Settings. The exercise will have the greatest impact if the story suits the audience. Thus, the story can be about a particular division of the company (Marketing, Research & Development, Manufacturing, etc.) and can even name particular employees as characters.

For Non-Business Settings. The example in Figure 3.4.1 has a business ring to it. You may wish to create new stories more relevant to the concerns of the group. Because the stories are brief, you'll probably find this easy to do.

For Schools. For this exercise, participants must be competent readers, and the story should be appropriate to the group. One quick way to come up with a story is to extract one from a story book. *Aesop's Fables* work well. Replace a few phrases with blanks, to be filled in by nonsense words.

Other Options

Quick Versions. The exercise will still have an impact if you use the words alone, without any stories to support them. Simply ask participants to pronounce the words in Figure 3.4.2, perhaps by going around the table. Different people will pronounce the same word in very different ways. Some will even add meaning and structure where none exists. For example, "tkeldifleowdnd" may become "Took a little fall. Oh, darned!" Another variation: You can require that participants create a *complete sentence* from each nonsense word. In a business environment, you can require that participants generate a *new product or service* from each nonsense word.

Other Variations. If time allows, have participants create their own nonsense words, rules, and sentences. This task can be assigned to a small group. Again, the more relevant the material, the greater the impact of the exercise.

Data Collection

This task is normally done aloud, so data collection can be difficult. If you choose to have participants write part of the exercise, Form 3.4.1 may be helpful.

FOLLOW-UP

Discussion Questions

1) Can people pronounce "unpronounceable" words, when given permission to do so? Why do you think this is possible?
2) The words in this exercise are ambiguous. How do ambiguous stimuli help (or hurt) the creative process?
3) What other effects do ambiguous stimuli have? How do they make you feel?
4) Do you encounter ambiguous stimuli at work? What effect do they have on you?
5) What have you learned from this exercise?

Debriefing

Many people are afraid of ambiguous stimuli, not because ambiguity is a real threat, but because it accelerates "generative" processes. When lots of ideas are competing simultaneously in our heads, we often feel confused and frustrated. With new ideas emerging from this confusion—not all of them especially valuable—we know we're at risk if we try to share our new ideas with colleagues and friends. In other words, ambiguity actually facilitates the creative process (see Section 2.2 and Chapter 7), but our social environment has taught many of us to fear ambiguous stimuli. An environment that gives us more "permission" to preserve and share new ideas can reduce the fear, and, as we'll see later, we can even use ambiguous stimuli deliberately to facilitate creative thinking throughout the day.

Long-Term Follow-Up

Long-term follow-up isn't needed for this exercise. The Workplace Challenge (Section 3.6) includes suggestions for following-up on all of the exercises in this section.

COMMENTS

Even simplified versions of this exercise (see *Quick Versions,* above) will make the point. If you use the story format, you may want to take some extra time to create your own stories. Best of all, have the participants do it. The more relevant the material, the more successful the exercise will be.

Figure 3.4.1. Story Format. Photocopy, and then separate the story portions.

HOW PAT GOT PROMOTED
FROM A MAIL-ROOM JOB TO THE
PRESIDENCY OF THE COMPANY

Pat had been a stamp-licker in the mail room for fourteen years. One day, when Pat went outside for a Twinkie break, a limousine carrying the President of the company ran over Pat's toes. This was a turning point in Pat's career. Pat exclaimed—well, shouted actually, "_____!"

Pat's best friend, Sal, was a very, very close friend—if you know what I mean—of Jo, who was the President's trusted Senior Executive Assistant, and who also happened to be the one who actually did all of the President's work. Jo's toes had also been run over recently, so Jo was only too happy to work with Sal and Pat to replace the President. Jo didn't want the job, because Jo was too smart for that. So they made a plan, which Jo, always the joker, called "The _____ Plan."

The Plan involved the usual stuff: a phony memo, a rumor about impending layoffs, some anonymous e-mail messages about the President's dietary preferences, and a brilliant suggestion from Pat—deposited into the Suggestion Box in the mail room—that saved the company from financial ruin. The President, understandably upset by all this, could only comment, "_____."
(After all, the President had used the same technique to become President just a few years before.)

The same day Pat's name was placed on the President's office door, Pat thanked Sal and Jo in a most unusual way—yes, that's right, by _____. Wow, what a mess!

Now Jo still runs the company, and Pat has fun running over the toes of people who work in the mail room. The moral of the story, of course, is _____.

Figure 3.4.2. Nonsense Words. Copy and distribute,
or display on an overhead projector.

1
okcceljalsfjeeijenc

2
ynnwhilzokoooehodwhsqd

3
voenslwugawneifhslree

4
wovnensownghisdyehslei

5
awynvmroheahehseralsjer

Participant's Notes and Evaluation
Exercise: "The Srtcdjgjklered Game"

Please turn the following nonsense words into full sentences, using the guidelines given to you by your trainer.

1. okcceljalsfjeeijenc

2. ynnwhilzokoooehodwhsqd

3. voenslwugawneifhslree

4. wovnensownghisdyehslei

5. awynvmroheahehseralsjer

Did these ambiguous stimuli force you to be "creative"? Yes ☐ No ☐ How?

To share data or comments with the author, fax this form to 619-436-4490.

*From **Creativity Games for Trainers**, by Dr. Robert Epstein. E-mail address: repstein@rohan.sdsu.edu.*

"The Srtcdjgjklered Game" *(Continued)*

Participant's name and contact information (optional):

_____

_____

_____

_____

Organization:

_____

_____

Position:

_____

_____

Date:

_____

_____

Trainer:

_____

_____

Value of the exercise:

LOW   ☐   ☐   ☐   ☐   ☐   HIGH

Suggestions for improving the exercise:

_____

_____

_____

_____

_____

EXERCISE: DESIGN CHALLENGE

BASICS

Objective

To further reinforce the belief that everyone is creative by having the participants themselves design an exercise that makes this point.

Brief Description

Participants are asked to spend a few minutes designing another exercise along the lines of the previous exercises in this chapter. They then carry out the new exercise. They may require the trainer to participate.

Materials and Supplies

They may use (a) any of the materials and supplies from the previous exercises in this chapter and (b) any additional materials, objects, or supplies that are present in the room.

Time Requirement

Minimum: 25 minutes. Maximum: 90 minutes.

PROCEDURE

Basic Procedure

Trainer: "In the exercises we've just completed, we've seen that every one of us has enormous creative potential. Now comes the next step: to begin to use this potential in a constructive way. Your task now is to design a new exercise that will further demonstrate what we have learned—an exercise that will show how enormously creative everyone can be. You'll have ten minutes in which to design this new task. Here are some guidelines: (a) you can make use of any of the objects and materials that we've used in previous exercises; (b) you can make use of any other objects or materials in this room; (c) you can assign people to different roles and send people out of the room, as necessary; (d) you can use me as one of the participants in this new exercise. After the ten-minute design period is over, you'll have an additional ten minutes in which to conduct the exercise. After that, a representative from your group will lead us all in a short debriefing to evaluate the outcome of the new exercise and to see whether your goals have been met."

Customizing the Procedure

For Small Groups. Small groups can be broken up into teams of approximately five people each. Each team should design its own exercise. If time allows, each team should be allowed to conduct the exercise it has designed, using the trainer and the other teams as participants.

For Large Groups. In a large auditorium where time is limited, a single team should be assembled, and that group should design an exercise for the rest of the audience. The team may need to leave the room to design the exercise. Alternatively, the larger group can be given a break while the team creates its design.

For Non-Business Settings. The trainer may wish to restrict the exercise to an area of creativity which is pertinent to the particular organizational setting. For example, in an exercise with hospital staff: "Be sure that your exercise uses objects, real or imagined, that might be used in a hospital setting."

For Schools or Homes. The trainer or teacher should lead the children in the design of the new exercise, eliciting suggestions and comments from them. With young children, the trainer should have a new exercise in mind before eliciting any feedback.

Other Options

As noted earlier, trainers should feel free to experiment with the way they conduct all Design Challenge exercises. One approach of special value: "Now I'm going to ask you to design an entirely new exercise, and I'm going to try some parameters that I've never used before. In other words, I'm going to be creative today—I'm going to take a risk—and I believe we'll all benefit from the experience, even if the outcome isn't entirely 'successful' in the usual sense of that term. Here's what I'd like you to do...."

It's not necessary to complete all three of the exercises in this section before beginning the Design Challenge, but at least one and preferably two others should be completed first.

Data Collection

The trainer may wish to use or modify Form A.3 in the Appendix of this book (p. 261).

FOLLOW-UP

Discussion Questions

1) What was the goal of this exercise? Did we reach that goal? Why or why not?
2) How could this exercise be improved?

3) What did this exercise teach us, if anything?

4) How can we relate the outcome of this exercise to the outcomes of the previous exercises in this chapter?

5) Is everyone creative? Have your views on this issue changed at all since we began this series of exercises?

Debriefing

Trainer (modify as appropriate): "This last exercise, which you designed yourselves, has, I hope, taken us to a new level in our understanding of the creative process. In short, it tells us that the more we learn about creativity, the more creative we can become. We have the ability to create methods and tools and procedures that make us more creative—every one of us, no matter what our position in the organization. Our next exercise will allow us to focus more directly on the organization itself."

Long-Term Follow-Up

This exercise does not require a long-term follow-up. If, however, there has been a dramatic result—a surprising or significant example of creativity, for example—that result should be preserved and posted so people will remember it and refer back to it. The point is to remind people how much creativity is valued in the organization.

COMMENTS

Trainers need to ensure: (a) that everyone gets a chance to participate, (b) that the exercise is fun and upbeat, and (c) that time limits are respected. A group-run exercise may overlook these requirements, so the trainer may need to intervene. If several exercises are to be conducted, the trainer will need to schedule breaks.

EXERCISE:
WORKPLACE CHALLENGE

BASICS

Objective

To extend the lessons of the previous exercises in this chapter to specific organizational settings.

Brief Description

Participants are asked to design an application, procedure, or policy (a) that is based on principles, methods, or outcomes from previous exercises in this chapter and (b) that has specific benefits for their particular workplaces.

Required Materials and Supplies

Writing materials.

Optional Materials and Supplies

Large, blank sheets of paper (without lines) should be available to encourage people to make diagrams or drawings. Word processors may be helpful in some settings.

Time Requirement

Minimum: 20 minutes. Maximum: 1 hour.

PROCEDURE

Basic Procedure

Trainer (modify as appropriate): "Our next step is to try to extend what we've learned to our particular organizational setting. If everyone is creative—and let's stay with this as our working assumption—how can we improve our workplace to take advantage of that fact? What policies or procedures might we change? How might we improve the work environment? How might we change or improve our training procedures? What other changes might we make? What outcomes—positive and negative—might we expect to result from such changes?

"Let's take ten minutes to sketch out our ideas. In the spirit of the exercises we've just completed, try to 'stay loose.' Don't be overly concerned just yet about the practicality of your suggestions. Don't think too much about budget. Just think, 'How might my organization be improved to take advantage of the fact that *everyone*—at every level of the organization—might have enormous creative potential that's not currently being tapped?' After ten minutes have passed, I'll ask some of you to share your ideas with the group, and we'll discuss them together. Any questions?"

Customizing the Procedure

For Small Groups. In a small group, everyone should be given an opportunity to present his or her ideas. The trainer should emphasize the value of every idea, no matter how impractical. *After* all of the ideas have been presented, the group can begin the task of assessing their feasibility and value.

For Large Groups. In a large group, everyone can sketch out ideas on paper, but the trainer will be able to call on only a few people to present them to the group.

For Non-Business Settings. Key concerns: (a) feasibility of implementation, (b) possible benefits and outcomes, and (c) special areas of concern.

For Schools or Homes. Children may need close supervision by the trainer or teacher.

Other Options

Participants might be allowed to work together in teams (although see the caveats in Chapter 8 of this volume). Where an audience includes members of different organizations, the trainer should make sure that each organization is given some consideration.

Data Collection

Trainers may wish to use or modify Form A.1 in the Appendix of this volume (p. 261).

FOLLOW-UP

Discussion Questions

1) Has the creative potential in your organization been tapped to its full extent? How have you tapped this potential so far?

2) Do cost-effective methods exist for tapping the creativity in your organization more fully? Describe some methods.

3) Do the people in your organization believe that they are creative? If not, how might you convince them?

4) Does your organization currently stifle creativity in some ways? How so?

5) Will promoting creativity in your organization be cost-effective? What's the downside? What's the upside?

6) How might creativity be important to your organization's survival?

Debriefing

Trainer (modify as appropriate): "It can be easy and inexpensive to promote creativity in an organization. In settings in which creativity is discouraged and procedures are long-entrenched, promoting creativity can be more difficult. Promoting creativity can mean new costs. It can also mean living with a higher degree of chaos and uncertainty. But stifling creativity will, long-term, almost certainly mean the premature destruction of an organization. An organization that does not foster creativity will have difficulty responding to a changing world."

Long-Term Follow-Up

Workplace Challenges should, whenever possible, be followed up. The trainer should encourage participants to complete and return Form A.2 (or some equivalent) in the Appendix of this volume (p. 261) thirty days after the completion of training. If possible, trainers should contact participants who don't return the forms on their own. A brief telephone interview will allow trainers to complete the form. Trainers should use the replies to evaluate and improve their own training procedures. The replies will also furnish examples of successes and failures that can be used in future training. Participants who expect some form of follow-up are more likely to implement material that they have mastered in training. Without follow-up, training often has little more than entertainment value.

COMMENTS

Some participants may choose to focus on an education issue: How can we convince the people in our organization that every one of them has creative contributions to make? Others may focus on practical issues: How can we tap the creative potential in our organization to cut costs, improve productivity, improve quality, and improve profitability? Participants should be allowed to choose their own emphasis. At this stage of training, participants should not be expected to solve every problem in their organization but rather to appreciate the fact that *a large number of potentially valuable solutions can easily be generated.*

CREATIVITY:
GENERAL DEBRIEFING

If you haven't used all five of the exercises in Chapter 3, you may want to rely on the relevant debriefing sections. If you're conducting a more comprehensive training session and you've conducted all five of the exercises, here are some suggestions for summarizing, for generating further discussion, and for wrapping up this portion of the training.

SUMMARY

Here's what a producer told me when I started writing radio commentaries a few years ago: "Tell 'em (yes, he said *'em,* not *them)* what you're gonna say, then say it, then tell 'em what you just said." That's pretty good advice for any teacher. You started your training session by telling people that everyone is creative; then you stepped your participants through some exercises to demonstrate the point; then you asked them to create their own exercise to demonstrate the point; then you asked them to extend this lesson to their work environment. Now, tell 'em what they've learned:

- **Generative processes** operate all the time in everyone. These processes underlie all creativity.

- Most of us were taught to ignore the **constant flow of new ideas** that our brains are generating, but we can learn to **pay attention** to this flow, just as we did when we were children.

- The **daydream** is a powerful, simple reminder that this creative flow exists in every one of us. Night dreams are also impressive wells of creativity. You don't have to look far to find your creative potential.

- Working together, we were able to **design our own exercise** to show how creative we are, and we've even taken a step toward applying what we've learned to the workplace.

You may wish to review transparencies from Section 2.1 (especially Figure 2.1.3) at this point.

FURTHER DISCUSSION

If you've not already exhausted the discussion questions listed at the end of each of the previous chapters in this section, this would be a good time to ask them. Your discussion at this point should try to draw out any reservations or concerns people have. Learn about these early, so that you can customize later exercises to suit people's needs. If the particular group you're working with is not especially responsive, try to raise some sensitive issues for them:

- Okay, we all dream and daydream, we can all sell Zorks, and we can all get creative when faced with nonsense words. How will this help us get our jobs done? How will this help our organization? How will this improve our lives?

- Sure, here in this sheltered environment, we're allow to get a little crazy, but what about back at the office? No one seems to value creativity where it really counts, so what's the point?

- If you're crazy enough to tell people about a good idea, it's bound to get stolen. Someone else will take credit for it, so why should I waste my time?

- If you try to get creative in our organization, you'll be ridiculed.

- There's no point being creative, because we don't have the resources to develop any new ideas right now. The inspiration is only ten percent of the effort; who's going to finance the other ninety percent?

- So far we've only been speaking in generalities. How, specifically, can we enhance and direct creativity in our organization?

WRAP-UP

At this point you may be wrapping up the first half-day of a full two-day training session on creativity. In your closing remarks, be clear about what the group has achieved thus far and about what you'll work to achieve in the next session. Ideally, refer to an outline that maps out your entire training plan, and show people where they are on the map. When you give people a *framework* for learning, the learning is much easier.

CHAPTER 4

"CAPTURING" GAMES:
WHY THE BED,
THE BATH,
AND THE BUS?

CAPTURING: ORIENTATION

He had gone to sleep that night thinking, as usual, about a difficult problem in cell biology that had bothered him for years. But this night was to be different. In the early morning hours, he awoke suddenly with the realization that he had just *solved* this vexing problem. He groped in the dark until he found the pad and pen near his bed. Groggy and excited, he sketched out the solution, dropped the pad on the floor, and, with a great sense of accomplishment, went back to sleep.

Unfortunately, when he finally awoke to the morning sun, he found that his notes were entirely illegible—and that he couldn't remember the solution! Had he just imagined this remarkable solution, or had it been real?

Fortunately for the world, the next night Dr. Loewi had the same informative dream, and this time he took no chances. He pulled on his clothes and drove straight to his laboratory. He won a Nobel Prize for the work he began that night, and he helped advance our knowledge of cell function considerably.

Pulling on your pants in the middle of the night is an extreme form of what I call "capturing"—the practice of preserving new ideas as they occur. *All* of the people that society calls "creative" have extensive capturing skills. The know *when and where* good ideas occur to them, and they stand ready to preserve them. They use recording devices—sketch pads, napkins, tape recorders, and computers—to aid them. They understand that new ideas are *fragile and fleeting;* you must preserve them at the moment they occur, or, like our dreams, they will likely disappear forever.

It may be that the *only* significant difference between "creative" people and the rest of us is that the creative types have better capturing skills. That's a weighty proposition, to be sure, but generativity research suggests that it's true.

Creative people seek out places and times that allow them to pay attention to the creative flow with minimal distraction. The "Three Bs of Creativity"—the Bed, the Bath, and the Bus—work well for many, but other people take more elaborate measures. In the early 1980s I was invited by Dr. Edwin Land, inventor of the Polaroid Camera, to speak about creativity at his new research center, the Rowland Institute. A Japanese garden ran the entire length of the center of the building, under hundreds of skylights. Stone paths snaked their way among the serene trees and bushes. He explained that the garden helped him stay creative. He had built, in effect, a multi-million dollar capturing device.

In the exercises that follow, participants will learn how fleeting new ideas can be ("The Random Doodles Game"). They will build their own (inexpensive!) capturing machines with the materials on-hand ("Building a Better Capturing Machine"). And they will learn about suggestion systems that can help promote capturing in organizational settings ("The Anonymous Suggestion Game"). Then, through the Design and Workplace Challenges, they'll design their own capturing exercise, and they'll have an opportunity to apply what they've learned to the needs of their own workplace.

EXERCISE: "THE RANDOM DOODLES GAME"

BASICS

Objective

To show how difficult it is to preserve new ideas unless we record them immediately.

Brief Description

Participants generate random doodles (or numbers or nonsense syllables) and then try to remember them, with or without the benefit of a memorandum.

Materials and Supplies

This exercise can be conducted in a number of different ways. I'll recommend one simple arrangement below. For this, you need only a standard large pad (the flipchart type) mounted on an easel, some markers, and some strong tape (masking tape will do). Figure 4.2.1 shows a format you may want to use to prepare the flipchart pages before you begin. The pages do not need to be prepared in advance, however. Warning: The paper needs to be sufficiently opaque so that writing doesn't easily show through from the pages below. A common black-board can be used instead, or, in a small group, sheets of paper will suffice. Various options are discussed below. A stopwatch would also be helpful.

Time Requirement

Minimum: 15 minutes. Maximum: 30 minutes.

PROCEDURE

Basic Procedure

Trainer (modify as needed): "New ideas surge through our heads throughout the day. Some have value, some do not. But unless we capture them, we'll never really know. New ideas are fleeting; they disappear as rapidly as they occur, and they often do not return. Artists, writers, composers, and inventors know this all too well. That's why they walk around with pads and tape recorders, jot notes on napkins and scraps of newspaper, and panic when they can't find a pen. Old ideas are fairly easy to remember; new ideas are difficult to remember unless we record them. Perhaps the main difference between people we call 'creative' and the rest of us is that the 'creative' types have excellent *capturing* skills. Let's see how this works."

The trainer now selects one or two volunteers. With two volunteers, two easels should be set up in the front of the room, and both volunteers should draw at the same time. The instructions below will assume that two people are drawing. With enough easels, you can have as many artists as you like.

Trainer: "I'd like you now to draw some items for me. Some you've heard of, and some will probably be new to you. If you've never heard of the object, just use your imagination. That's why we call this exercise the 'Doodle Game.' When I tell you the name of the object, write that name in the appropriate spot at the top of the page; then write it again in large letters in the center of the page; then write it a third time in the appropriate spot on the bottom portion of the page. Then make your drawing in the space at the top of the page. You'll have *thirty seconds* to make each drawing. Any questions? Okay, here is the first object."

The trainer then reads a list of words, some real and some nonsensical. I suggest that you have people make *six* drawings, *four* from nonsense syllables. For the real words, feel free to use the names of objects that are common to the work environment. Here are some suggested objects:

Real	**Imaginary**	
TREE	ORK	JUB
HOUSE	ZIL	NID
CAR	GAK	EEF
DOG	YUG	KIF
GIRL	VEB	MIP
TABLE	ILM	ORZ

After each drawing is complete, the trainer (and, if needed, a helper from the audience) should cover each drawing by folding the sheet into thirds, fanfold style, as shown below. The sheet should be taped securely at the top.

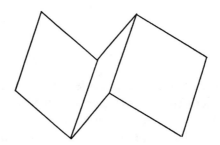

When all of the drawings have been completed and covered as shown, the trainer should arrange for a delay in the proceedings. Although this delay is not necessary, the longer the delay, the more dramatic the effect will be. Depending on the circumstances, the trainer can call a short break or conduct a brief discussion about capturing (see Section 4.1 for material) during the delay. If you're going to talk about capturing, it's important that you *not* refer to the drawings that were just made by the volunteers.

After a delay of five to ten minutes, the trainer should recall the volunteers to the easels and continue: "Let's see how well you remember what you've drawn. I'm going to read the object names to you in a different order than I said them a little while ago. After I name an object, you'll have thirty seconds to draw that object again, this time on the lower third of each sheet. No peeking at what you drew before. Any questions? Okay, here are is the first object."

The trainer repeats the object names in a new order, making sure that the volunteers are making their new drawings on the appropriate sheets.

Finally, when all the drawings are complete, the tape is removed and the old and new drawings are compared.

For real objects, the old and new drawings will usually be similar. For imaginary objects, you will probably find little or no correspondence between the old and new drawings. New ideas are often difficult to remember, especially when there is no frame of reference in which to remember them. If anything, it should be easier to remember the doodles in this exercise than to remember many of the new ideas we have in the real world. In the exercise, participants have a chance to *draw* their doodles; in the real world, ideas come and go in our heads and never even see the light of day.

Customizing the Procedure

For Small Groups. In a small group, all of the participants can draw directly on letter-sized sheets of paper and then share the results.

For Large Groups. In a very large group, you may want to have between two and four easels going at the same time. The easels should be positioned to give everyone a clear view of at least one "artist."

For Non-Business Settings. The real objects should be selected to suit the audience and occasion.

For Schools or Homes. The exercise works well in many different settings. For children, however, you might want to shorten the exercise considerably.

Other Options

This exercise can be done in many different ways. The way I've described it above is actually fairly elaborate. You can make the same point by having everyone in the group draw a doodle, cover it, and then, some time later, try to draw it again. It's tough to do! (Try it and see!)

You need not even use drawings. You can have people make up their own nonsense syllables and try to remember them later, or you can have them generate random numbers and try to remember them. The point is that any novel behavior you ask people to generate will be very difficult for them to remember. Mozart and Beethoven had the same problem.

If easels and flipcharts are unavailable, you can use a blackboard (carefully covering the "before" drawings with poster-board taped to the blackboard) or even sheets of letter-sized paper.

One technical point: There's an easy way to compare *unaided recall* of a novel idea to *aided recall* of a novel idea. You've got a *before* doodle (the original recording) and an *after* doodle (unaided recall). Now ask the participant to *draw a copy* of the original drawing (aided recall), and compare that drawing to the after doodle. Which is the more faithful replica of the original idea?

Data Collection

This exercise can yield some interesting drawings, showing dramatically in some cases how difficult it can be to remember novel ideas. You may want to use Form 4.2.1 or Figure 4.2.1 to help you collect some interesting examples of before and after drawings.

FOLLOW-UP

Discussion Questions

1) Why do you think novel ideas are so difficult to remember?
2) Can you think of a time when a great idea occurred to you and then disappeared, never to return? (It's interesting that we can often remember the incident but not the idea.)
3) What did you learn from this exercise?

Debriefing

In this exercise, we see that people have a much easier time reproducing old ideas than they have reproducing new ones. Novel ideas are like rabbits: They move swiftly through the underbrush, and before you know it, they're gone. Not every new idea has value, of course, but if you want to produce more genuinely creative material, you need to start with a larger pool of novel ideas. So preserve first, and evaluate later.

Long-Term Follow-Up

In the 1930s an English psychologist told people stories and then let some time pass before asking them to repeat the stories—hours, weeks, months, even years. If it suits your schedule and your needs, you might find value in asking your participants to try to draw an "ork" or a "veb" or an "ilm" after days or weeks have passed. It's a quick and easy test, and it drives home the point. Recall for novel ideas fades quickly.

COMMENTS

This exercise, like virtually all exercises, depends on the good faith efforts of the participants—and the skill and experience of the trainer! If you ask someone to draw an "ilm," and she proceeds to draw a hamburger, you may need to coach her a bit: "Let's start that one over on a clean sheet. I can't tell you exactly what an *ilm* is, but I can tell you that it's *not* a hamburger. An *ilm* is something new and strange. Use your imagination and try again."

Figure 4.2.1. *Flipchart format (optional). Each page should be divided into thirds. The top portion is for the "before" drawing, the middle portion contains the name of the object (supplied by the trainer), and the bottom portion is for the "after" drawing. After the top drawing is completed, the page should immediately be folded upward, fanfold style, so that Line 3 (below) meets the top of the page (Line 1). This will cover the first drawing and expose the bottom third of the paper, which is now ready for the "after" drawing.*

LINE 1   BEFORE: OBJECT

LINE 2

OBJECT

LINE 3   AFTER: OBJECT

Participant's Notes and Evaluation
Exercise: "The Random Doodles Game"

Please sketch some of the before and after drawings you made in this exercise:

	BEFORE	AFTER
Object:		
Object:		
Object:		
Object:		
Object:		

Did you have any difficulty trying to remember new patterns?   Yes ☐   No ☐   Any comments?

_____

_____

_____

_____

To share data or comments with the
author, fax this form to 619-436-4490.

*From **Creativity Games for Trainers**, by Dr. Robert*
Epstein. E-mail address: repstein@rohan.sdsu.edu.

"The Random Doodles Game" *(Continued)*

Participant's name and contact information (optional):

_____

_____

_____

_____

Organization:

_____

_____

Position:

_____

_____

Date:

_____

_____

Trainer:

_____

_____

Value of the exercise:

LOW   ☐   ☐   ☐   ☐   ☐   HIGH

Suggestions for improving the exercise:

_____

_____

_____

_____

_____

EXERCISE: "BUILDING A BETTER CAPTURING MACHINE"

BASICS

Objective

To show people how easily they can use the materials around them to capture new ideas.

Brief Description

Participants are asked to create "capturing machines"—devices that help them preserve new ideas—using whatever materials are on hand.

Materials and Supplies

You have many options here. At one extreme, you can conduct this exercise with *no* special materials or supplies. You can force your participants to rely on whatever happens to be at hand. In a barren room, this might not work very well, but it would still be worth doing (I believe in challenges, as you know by now!). I suggest collecting a large assortment of bizarre items for this exercise—anything but a pen and pad! This, too, provides a challenge, and it also makes the exercise more fun. If you expect to bring two volunteers to the front of the room (see below), then, for dramatic effect, before the exercise begins you should create two piles of the strange objects and cover each pile with a cloth. Uncover them when you give the "Go" to begin constructing the first device.

Time Requirement

Minimum: 15 minutes. Maximum: 30 minutes.

PROCEDURE

Basic Procedure

Trainer (modify as needed): "During the next few minutes, I'm going to ask each of you to become inventors of a very special kind: inventors who invent devices that help them create more inventions. Specifically, I'm going to ask you to create devices that will allow you to capture new ideas that pop into your heads. You need to be able to capture such ideas 'on the fly,' as they occur, even if a paper and pencil are unavailable. So, our first ground rule is that paper, pencils, and pens are prohibited from this game. That's right—no felt-tip markers or pocket computers, either. No traditional writing implements, period. Our second rule is that you're going to have to act quickly, because new ideas are usually fleeting, and they can be difficult to remember."

At this point you might want to give an example of an on-the-fly capturing device. Feel free to borrow one of mine: At a wedding years ago I had a pleasant chat with a woman sitting near me, and I asked for her phone number. Neither of us had a pen or paper, but there were plenty of napkins around. I said, "Okay, what's the number?" and proceeded to make small tear marks around the edge of the napkin—six tears for the number six, and so on, with a space between each number. I marked the starting point with a dab of mustard. Our eventual date was a disaster, but the capturing device worked like a charm.

Trainer: "I'd like two volunteers to come to the front of the room. The volunteers will have to restrict their construction activities to the specific materials I've provided for them. The rest of you can use anything in this room—except for traditional writing aids. Any questions? Is everyone ready? Okay, on my signal, you'll have *thirty seconds* in which to create your first capturing device. Ready, *Go!*"

After thirty seconds have passed, the trainer should spend a few minutes pointing out what the volunteers and some other members of the group have accomplished. The procedure should be repeated until everyone has built (or tried to build) about five devices.

Customizing the Procedure

For Small Groups. In a small group, everyone could conceivably use the objects provided by the trainer; however, the challenge is even greater if you leave most of the participants the task of locating their own materials.

For Large Groups. In a large auditorium where people can't easily change their seats, you might give the audience the option of sketching their machines on paper, perhaps using Form 4.3.1. Volunteers should still be brought to the front of the room to build the machines using the materials you've supplied.

For Non-Business Settings. This exercise is fun and informative in any setting. No special modifications are required for non-business settings.

For Schools or Homes. Children can't benefit from this exercise until they've developed what some psychologists call a "meta-memory"—that is, they need to have some idea about the limits of their own ability to remember things. I hesitate to attach an age to this ability, because children vary considerably in their abilities. The exercise is simple and fun, so there's no harm in trying it.

Other Options

You may want to have more volunteers in front of the room, each with a different collection of odd objects from which to build their machines. The audience, in this case, can simply watch rather than invent their own machines. You can also do the exercise in two phases: Have the volunteers build a couple of machines first, and then have the audience build their own devices with the materials they have on hand.

Data Collection

This is a mechanical, hands-on exercise, so it's difficult to collect data with paper and pencil. Your best bet is a videotape recorder. Form 4.3.1 can be used to record sketches of some of the machines, as well as to provide general feedback about the exercise.

FOLLOW-UP

Discussion Questions

1) How difficult is it to create a "capturing machine"?
2) Tell us about an interesting capturing machine that you've created in the past. What thought were you trying to preserve? Were you successful?
3) What did you learn from this exercise?

Debriefing

We all know how to make memoranda, but we tend to rely heavily on paper and pencil. In this exercise, we've pushed the envelope of creativity by having people create their own memory devices. Thus, we're using the creative process to help promote the creative process itself, because unless people have good capturing skills, the vast majority of good ideas are lost.

Long-Term Follow-Up

If your training sessions are not conducted in consecutive days, you can plan for some short-term follow-up fairly easily. Before one session ends, ask participants to take note of any new capturing machines they invent before the next training session. Better yet, give them a form or checklist to help them keep track. At the next session, ask them to describe their new machines to the group.

Some trainers routinely contact their trainees long after a session has ended (say, after thirty days). This is a great way to get feedback on the effectiveness of training and hence a great way to bring about continuous improvement in training methods. If this exercise has had an impact, your trainees should report some success at creating new capturing machines. What new ideas, if any, were they able to preserve for the organization? Even one idea of value will more than justify the training effort.

COMMENTS

Your choice of objects for the volunteers is an important factor in determining the success of this exercise. Modify your collection of objects to make the exercise as fun and as relevant as possible.

Participant's Notes and Evaluation
Exercise: "Building a Better Capturing Machine"

Please sketch or describe your new capturing machines:

1

2

3

4

5

Did you use any materials or items in ways that were new to you?   Yes ☐   No ☐   Please explain.

"Building a Better Capturing Machine" (Continued)

Participant's name and contact information (optional):

_____

_____

_____

_____

Organization:

_____

_____

Position:

_____

_____

Date:

_____

_____

Trainer:

_____

_____

Value of the exercise:

| LOW | ☐ | ☐ | ☐ | ☐ | ☐ | HIGH |

Suggestions for improving the exercise:

_____

_____

_____

_____

_____

EXERCISE: "THE ANONYMOUS SUGGESTION GAME"

BASICS

Objective

To show that people are usually more willing to express their new ideas when they can do so anonymously—that is, when the risk of ridicule or punishment is removed.

Brief Description

Participants make suggestions for improving the training session—either with or without the protection of anonymity.

Materials and Supplies

For this exercise, you will need to create two different survey forms—those that protect anonymity and those that don't. You may want to use Forms 4.4.1 and 4.4.2, if they suit your needs. If possible, have a paper shredder available in the front of the room. For added drama, keep the shredder hidden until it is needed near the end of the exercise (see below).

Time Requirement

Minimum: 15 minutes. Maximum: 30 minutes.

PROCEDURE

Basic Procedure

This is one of those "it's-not-what-it-seems" exercises. You'll see what that means shortly. Trainer (modify as necessary): "This next exercise serves several purposes, including a very practical one for me. I'm going to ask each of you to give me suggestions for improving this training seminar. Half of you will be able to do so anonymously, and half of you will need to put your names and contact information on the survey form. When you've completed the forms, I'll collect them. We'll tally them, and then we'll pick some forms at random to see if we can detect a difference in the kinds of comments people make with anomymity and without anonymity. My department head and I will review all of the sheets later to help plan future training sessions. Any questions?"

Form 4.4.1 (or equivalent) should be given to half the group and Form 4.4.2 (or equivalent) should be given to the other half.

When the forms have been completed, have an assistant or volunteer collect them and compile a quick tally of the *average number of suggestions made by members of each half of the group*. Form 4.4.3 should be used for this purpose; it contains instructions for completing the tallying, and, more important, it *masks* the suggestions people have made (simply cut out the box as indicated on the form). While the tallying is being done, the trainer can let the group stretch for a few minutes or can lead a discussion about the advantages and disadvantages of anonymity.

When the tallying is complete, the trainer should review it quickly. If the group is typical, people in the anonymous group will have made more suggestions (on the average) than people in the group without anonymity. (In a small group, outlying values can unfairly skew the mean; the more appropriate statistic is the median.)

Trainer (modify as appropriate): "The tallying is complete, and I must admit that I deliberately misled you. All I'd like to look at are the *number* of suggestions that were made in each of the groups. Do you think we'll find a different number of suggestions in the two groups? If we did look at the specific suggestions that were made, do you think they would differ in the two groups? Which suggestions are more candid (and what is the opposite of 'candid')? Which suggestions are more valuable to the organization? What are the key issues here?" (See further discussion questions below.)

There are different ways to end the exercise. Because you never actually intended to put individuals on the spot, it's a good idea, in front of the group, to shred the surveys that have the names on them. Better yet, shred all of the surveys, and keep the tally.

Customizing the Procedure

For Small Groups. In small groups, computing the means for each half of the group might produce a spurious result, because means are overly sensitive to outlying values. If your group has fewer than twenty members, you're probably better off with medians.

For Large Groups. For large groups you may need two or more assistants to tally the sheets. If you have the resources, create a form that can be read by a high-speed scanner, and let your computer do the scoring.

For Non-Business Settings. This exercise needs no special modifications for the non-business setting.

For Schools or Homes. To their credit, young children, generally speaking, are not afraid of having their ideas ridiculed by peers or authority figures. That fear is established during the grade-school years, when we "socialize" our children. This exercise is unlikely to produce group differences until children have passed this important but costly milestone.

Other Options

If you have suitable equipment, you may want to project the completed tally sheet onto a screen. Copying it onto a transparency is one easy way to accomplish this.

The task itself can be changed. Instead of having the group evaluate the trainer or training session, you can substitute almost any "sensitive" assignment: evaluating the boss, evaluating someone's appearance, commenting on someone sitting nearby, and so on. This is not as dangerous as it might seem, because the forms will actually be destroyed at the end of the exercise. All you're really interested in is the tally. The more sensitive the task, the larger the difference you can expect in the two groups.

One could conceivably take this exercise a step further than I have suggested. One could examine some of the statements on the forms, looking for signs of honesty, insight, creativity, innovation, and so on. This, too, can be done without great risk, simply by having your assistant black out the names and contact information on the sheets. With the anonymous forms in one pile and the expurgated forms in another, one could conduct an interesting comparison along many different dimensions. I can't honestly recommend this approach, because it does involve some risk of offending people, but don't let that discourage you.

Data Collection

The tally sheet (Form 4.4.3) provides one method of preserving some data. If you like, you can also distribute one of the general feedback forms included in the Appendix in this volume.

FOLLOW-UP

Discussion Questions

1) Do people respond differently when their anonymity is assured? How so?
2) Even assuming that people are more honest or creative when they can remain anonymous, a suggestion system that does not allow people to claim their good ideas would surely fail. Why?
3) What's wrong with a suggestion system that requires people to identify themselves?
4) What kind of suggestion system would best promote capturing?
5) Why are people often reluctant to contribute their ideas to the group?

Debriefing

Trainer (modify as necessary): "Suggestion systems are tricky. In fact, it's difficult in general to get people to contribute their best ideas to an organization. There are many reasons for this. For one thing, the very best ideas are worth a great deal of money; sometimes people think about striking out on their own, and sometimes they do exactly that. Also, people are afraid that their ideas will be stolen—or at least that someone else will take the credit, which is almost the same thing. People are afraid of ridicule: 'That's the most bubble-headed idea I've heard in years!' 'We wasted millions on that idea ten years ago! What hole did *you* crawl out of?' People are often certain that they'll be ignored, which is sometimes even more infuriating than being ridiculed. People are afraid to make waves, period—afraid that they'll be the first ones to drown.

"And yet the people who work for an organization are the source of all new ideas that flow into it. How do we encourage people to contribute on an ongoing basis?

"There are many ways to accomplish this. One simple way is to establish a suggestion system that promotes capturing: an anonymous suggestion system that allows people to claim their ideas if they wish. How you set this up—with two-part numbered suggestion forms, with special e-mail addresses and codes, with a bulletin board system—depends on your particular work environment."

Long-Term Follow-Up

At a thirty-day follow-up, the trainer may wish to determine whether participants have made any changes in the suggestion systems used in their work environments.

COMMENTS

What do you do if this exercise fails to produce the predicted result? I suggest being honest and then making the most of the situation. Say that, as far as you know, the predicted result is indeed the usual one, and then try to work with the group to account for the discrepancy: Were outlying points the culprits? Did some people predict the result and try to sabotage it? Is there something unique about this group or this environment that would predict a different outcome? In other words, work with the group to try to *learn something* from what happened. If nothing else, that might help you modify the exercise for the next group!

This exercise, needless to say, only glosses the surface of the difficulties involved in introducing new ideas into an organization. To an organization, a new idea is like a gold brick falling from the sky: Everyone wants to catch it, but no one wants to be crushed by it. And all but a few think that it's probably fool's gold, anyway.

A fuller understanding of the effects that different suggestion systems have on creative behavior would require an analysis of the "contingencies of reinforcement and punishment" that are inherent in each suggestion system. That analysis is beyond the scope of this volume.

Feedback Survey (Form 1)
Exercise: "The Anonymous Suggestion Game"

*Your name (required):*_____ *Telephone (required):*_____
*Other contact information:*_____

Please indicate ways in which this series of training sessions might be improved in the future:_____

1._____
_____

2._____
_____

3._____
_____

4._____
_____

5._____
_____

6._____
_____

7._____
_____

8._____
_____

9._____
_____

10._____
_____

To share data or comments with the author, fax this form to 619-436-4490.

*From **Creativity Games for Trainers**, by Dr. Robert Epstein. E-mail address: repstein@rohan.sdsu.edu.*

Feedback Survey (Form 2)
Exercise: "The Anonymous Suggestion Game"

Please indicate ways in which this series of training sessions might be improved in the future:

1. _____
_____

2. _____
_____

3. _____
_____

4. _____
_____

5. _____
_____

6. _____
_____

7. _____
_____

8. _____
_____

9. _____
_____

10. _____
_____

To share data or comments with the author, fax this form to 619-436-4490.

From Creativity Games for Trainers, by Dr. Robert Epstein. E-mail address: repstein@rohan.sdsu.edu.

Tally Sheet
"The Anonymous Suggestion Game"

Below, please tally the number of suggestions made on each of the two forms:

FORM 1 (PUBLIC)   FORM 2 (ANONYMOUS)

CUT OUT BOX

Mean =   Mean =

Median =   Median =

Trainer:_____ Site:_____ Date:_____

To share data or comments with the author, fax this form to 619-436-4490.

*From **Creativity Games for Trainers**, by Dr. Robert Epstein. E-mail address: repstein@rohan.sdsu.edu.*

EXERCISE: DESIGN CHALLENGE

BASICS

Objective

To further demonstrate the importance of capturing good ideas when they occur, in this case by having the participants themselves design an exercise that makes this point.

Brief Description

Participants are asked to spend a few minutes designing another exercise along the lines of the previous exercises in this chapter. They then carry out the new exercise. They may require the trainer to participate.

Materials and Supplies

They may use (a) any of the materials and supplies from the previous exercises in this chapter and (b) any additional materials, objects, or supplies that are present in the room.

Time Requirement

Minimum: 30 minutes. Maximum: 90 minutes.

PROCEDURE

Basic Procedure

Trainer: "In the exercises we've just completed, we've seen that new ideas are fleeting, that we benefit by arranging ways to 'capture' new ideas as they occur, that there are 'capturing machines' all around us, and that simple systems can be established to promote capturing in an organization. Now comes the next step: to begin to apply when we've learned. Your task now is to design a new exercise that will further demonstrate what we have learned—an exercise that will teach something about some aspect of capturing. You may focus on any aspect that you like. You'll have fifteen minutes in which to design this new task. Here are some guidelines: (a) you can make use of any of the objects and materials that we've used in previous exercises; (b) you can make use of any other objects or materials in this room; (c) you can assign people to different roles and send people out of the room, as necessary;

(d) you can use me as one of the participants in this new exercise. After the fifteen-minute design period is over, you'll have an additional ten minutes in which to conduct the exercise. After that, a representative from your team will lead us all in a short debriefing to evaluate the outcome of the new exercise and to see whether your goals have been met."

Customizing the Procedure

For Small Groups. Small groups can be broken up into teams of approximately five people each. Each team should design its own exercise. If time allows, each team should be allowed to conduct the exercise it has designed, using the trainer and the other teams as participants.

For Large Groups. In a large auditorium where time is limited, a single team should be assembled, and that group should design an exercise for the rest of the audience. The team may need to leave the room to design the exercise. Alternatively, the larger group can be given a break while the team creates its design.

For Non-Business Settings. The trainer may wish to restrict the exercise to capturing concerns that are unique to the particular organizational setting. For example, on an assembly line, it may be difficult for someone with a brilliant idea for improving efficiency on the line to stop and take notes.

For Schools or Homes. The trainer or teacher should lead the children in the design of the new exercise, eliciting suggestions and comments from them. With young children, the trainer should have a new exercise in mind before eliciting any feedback. As noted earlier, children need to have adequate "meta-memory" skills before they are likely to benefit from learning about capturing.

Other Options

Trainers should feel free to experiment with the way they conduct all Design Challenge exercises. See Section 3.5 for further suggestions.

It's not necessary to complete all three of the exercises in this section before beginning the Design Challenge, but at least one and preferably two others should be completed first.

Data Collection

The trainer may wish to use or modify Form A.3 in the Appendix of this book (p. 261).

FOLLOW-UP

Discussion Questions

1) What was the goal of this exercise? Did we reach that goal? Why or why not?
2) How could this exercise be improved?

3) What did this exercise teach us, if anything?

4) How can we relate the outcome of this exercise to the outcomes of the previous exercises in this chapter?

5) Why is capturing an important tool for promoting creativity? Have your views on this issue changed since we began this series of exercises?

Debriefing

The trainer should call on a member of the design group to offer comments or lead a brief discussion. The trainer may want to add: "This last exercise, which you designed yourselves, has, I hope, taken you a step further in our quest for creativity. It shows that you have the potential to design new ways to teach others how the creative process works—in particular, to teach others about the important role that capturing plays in the promotion of creativity."

Long-Term Follow-Up

This exercise does not require a long-term follow-up. If, however, there has been a dramatic result—a surprising or significant example of creativity, for example—that result should be preserved and posted so people will remember it and refer back to it. This guideline applies to all of the games in this volume.

COMMENTS

As usual, trainers need to ensure: (a) that everyone gets a chance to participate, (b) that the exercise is fun, and (c) that time limits are respected. If several exercises are to be conducted, the trainer will need to schedule breaks.

This exercise, like all of the Challenge exercises in this volume, puts a burden on the participants (and, perforce, on the trainer). It puts the pressure on to be creative—just like the real world often does. So the participants might conceivably *fail* and *feel frustrated*. Watch for signs of failure and frustration, and then *point them out* and *make them part of the training*. New ideas spring from failure (see Chapters 2 and 5); at the first signs of it, try to make people more aware of the essential role it's playing in the creative process.

EXERCISE:
WORKPLACE CHALLENGE

BASICS

Objective

To extend the lessons of the previous exercises in this chapter to specific organizational settings.

Brief Description

Participants are asked to design an application, procedure, or policy (a) that is based on principles, methods, or outcomes from previous exercises in this chapter and (b) that has specific benefits for their particular workplaces.

Required Materials and Supplies

Writing materials.

Optional Materials and Supplies

Large, blank sheets of paper (without lines) should be available to encourage people to make diagrams or drawings. Word processors may be helpful in some settings.

Time Requirement

Minimum: 20 minutes. Maximum: 1 hour.

PROCEDURE

Basic Procedure

Trainer (modify as appropriate): "Our next step is to try to extend what we've learned about capturing to our particular organizational setting. If capturing is essential for promoting creativity, how can we improve our workplace to take advantage of that fact? What policies or procedures might we change? How might we improve the work environment? How might we change or improve our training procedures? What other changes might we make? What outcomes—positive and negative—might we expect to result from such changes?

"Let's take ten minutes to sketch out our ideas. In the spirit of the exercises we've just completed, try to 'stay loose.' Don't be overly concerned just yet about the practicality of your suggestions. Don't think too much about budget or politics. Just think, 'How can we put capturing systems in place in every level of our organization?' After ten minutes have passed, I'll ask some of you to share your ideas with the group, and we'll discuss them together. Any questions?"

Customizing the Procedure

For Small Groups. In a small group, everyone should be given an opportunity to present his or her ideas. The trainer should emphasize the value of every idea, no matter how impractical. *After* all of the ideas have been presented, the group can begin the task of assessing their feasibility and value.

For Large Groups. In a large group, everyone can sketch out ideas on paper, but the trainer will be able to call on only a few people to present their ideas to the group.

For Non-Business Settings. Key concerns: (a) feasibility of implementation, (b) possible benefits and outcomes, and (c) special areas of concern.

For Schools or Homes. The teacher may wish to lead a discussion about "how we can get ourselves to be more creative."

Other Options

Participants should be allowed to work together in small teams (although see the caveats in Chapter 8 of this volume). Where an audience includes members of different organizations, the trainer should make sure that each organization is given some consideration.

As usual, where the dollar value of ideas is of special importance, the trainer may want to divide the discussion into two parts: First, ideas should be presented, without judgment or evaluation, and listed on a blackboard or easel. Second, ideas should be prioritized, taking into account (a) feasibility of implementation, (b) dollar value to the organization, (c) other possible benefits, and (d) special areas of concern.

Data Collection

Trainers may wish to modify Form A.1 in the Appendix of this volume (p. 261).

FOLLOW-UP

Discussion Questions

1) To what extent does your workplace currently promote good capturing?

2) What kinds of supplies would help preserve the good ideas that occur to people in your organization?

3) Does your organization currently have a suggestion system of some sort? How does it work, and is it effective?

4) Does your organization currently provide special times or places that are conducive to creativity? Is this feasible?

Debriefing

You may want to have a member of the team lead a brief discussion about the proposals that were made by members of the team. You may want to add: "Capturing is the most important key to promoting creativity in an organization. It doesn't actually facilitate the creative process, but it takes advantage of the enormous creativity that already exists. It contains a number of elements, many of which are reflected in the proposals you have made: (1) training people to capture their new ideas, (2) providing supplies—like idea software and idea folders—to help people preserve their ideas, (3) providing times and places that allow people to focus on their creative energies without distraction, and (4) providing risk-free suggestion systems (appropriate 'contingencies of reinforcement') that encourage people to share their ideas with the organization."

Long-Term Follow-Up

As noted earlier, Workplace Challenges should, whenever possible, be followed up. Thirty days after the completion of training, the trainer should encourage participants to complete and return a form that reports on their progress, if any, in implementing their ideas; Form A.2 in the Appendix of this volume (p. 261) can be used or modified for this purpose. If possible, trainers should contact participants who don't return the forms on their own. A brief telephone interview will allow trainers to complete the form. Trainers should use the replies to evaluate and improve their own training procedures. The replies will also furnish examples of successes and failures that can be used in future training. Participants who expect some form of follow-up are more likely to implement material that they have mastered in training. Without follow-up, training often has little more than entertainment value.

COMMENTS

Some participants will be overly concerned with feasibility issues when asked to meet a Workplace Challenge. How, they ask, can we contemplate sweeping changes in policies and procedures when we can't even get new pencils?

If such a concern is evident in your group, you'll need to answer it. If you don't, people will feel that you're wasting their time. Fortunately, the question has a straightforward answer in the context of these games: "Even if change seems unlikely, you can surely *contemplate* it. That's what creativity is all about, and that's what we're here to learn. The exercise alone is valuable, but this is more than just an exercise. All change starts with someone's idea. *Contemplating* change is an essential step toward producing change. If you don't contemplate it, it can't happen. This small act of creativity raises the probability of change from *zero* to some small finite value. That's a shift of infinite magnitude, and infinity, in anyone's book, is a significant number."

CAPTURING:
GENERAL DEBRIEFING

In the games we've just completed, we've learned how critically important it is to preserve good ideas as soon as they occur. The skills that help us achieve this are called "capturing" skills. Such skills are probably the only thing that separates so-called creative people from the rest of us.

As school children, most of us learned to ignore the flow of new ideas that continuously courses through our brains. When we learn to attend to this flow, we've taken a critical step toward greater creativity. When we learn to preserve parts of this flow, we've taken another important step.

Here are some of the ideas we explored in this portion of our training:

- New ideas are generally fleeting and fragile. We explored that concept in the "Doodles" exercise.

- We can use the materials around us to help us capture new ideas as they occur. We constructed some simple capturing devices in our second exercise.

- People are often reluctant to preserve and share their new ideas with others in an organization. In our third exercise, we explored the value of using anonymous suggestion systems to encourage people to capture and share new ideas in an organization.

- Our capturing efforts will be more successful if we place ourselves in settings—such as the Bed, the Bath, and the Bus—that allow us to pay attention, with minimal distraction, to our creative thoughts.

CHAPTER 5

"CHALLENGING" GAMES: CAN FAILURE LEAD TO SUCCESS?

CHALLENGING:
ORIENTATION

Thomas Edison tried twenty thousand different materials before finding one that was even marginally suitable to serve as a lightbulb filament. So if you're failing, you're in good company.

Failure—also known as "extinction" or "non-reinforcement"—has many effects, and none of them feels very good. But one outcome of failure is creativity, so it may be worth it for us to put up with a few bad feelings.

In laboratory studies, extinction produces at least five effects: (1) the gradual disappearance of the previously successful behavior (we eventually "give up"), (2) a temporary increase in the force of that behavior (we "try harder"), (3) the appearance of variations in the form of that behavior, (4) an increase in emotional behavior (we get "frustrated"), and (5) the appearance of other behaviors that were successful in the past in situations similar to the present one. The last effect, called *resurgence*, helps spur creativity by getting many behaviors to compete with each other, resulting in new sequences and new forms of behavior. The frustration you feel during extinction is probably the subjective side of this dynamic competition; it's the way you feel when many neural systems are lit up simultaneously.

You can still be creative, of course, without experiencing any significant failure; generative mechanisms operate continuously no matter what you do. But dramatic instances of creativity are often born of the agony of defeat, because there's nothing like defeat to get the generative apparatus operating in high gear. Evolution has, quite sensibly, equipped our nervous systems so that when we fail, *everything that we've ever done in our lives that has helped us in similar situations* will tend to recur. In our nervous systems, the cavalry actually come to our rescue.

Challenging is the practice of deliberately exposing yourself or others to difficult problems in order to foster creativity. Challenges are great spurs to the creative process, for the reasons we've discussed.

Failure has value, but if you suggest that everyone in your organization should be made to fail regularly, your popularity will decline. The trick is to introduce a *manageable and predictable* degree of failure to your daily operations, which we will call a Controlled Failure System. In such a system, (1) failure is tolerated by management, (2) the level of risk is limited, and (3) the level of frustration is controlled. How you establish such systems will depend on your particular organization and problems.

In the exercises that follow, we'll explore three aspects of failure. In the first exercise, "The Not-for-the-Fainthearted Game," we'll see firsthand the almost magical effect that extinction has on the creative process. In the second exercise, "The ABCs of Creativity," we'll learn that success—the flip side of failure—can actually impede our ability to solve simple problems. In the third exercise, "The Ultimate Challenge Game," we'll explore the value of "open-ended problems"—problems that have an infinite number of solutions—in spurring creativity. In the Design and Workplace Challenges that follow, participants will have a chance to apply what they've learned.

EXERCISE: "THE NOT-FOR-THE-FAINTHEARTED GAME"

BASICS

Objective

To show the important role that failure ("extinction") plays in the emergence of novel behavior.

Brief Description

In this high-energy exercise, the entire group uses a "shaping" procedure to teach a volunteer to do something and then allows the volunteer to "fail" for a few minutes. As a warm-up, the trainer has the group use the shaping procedure to teach him or her to do something.

Materials and Supplies

No special materials or supplies are needed.

Time Requirement

Minimum: 20 minutes. Maximum: 40 minutes.

PROCEDURE

Basic Procedure

Part One: "Embarrass the Trainer." For training purposes, you should ignore the name that's given to this exercise in the beginning of the chapter. Instead, continue as follows:

Trainer: "We're going to begin a new game, which, unfortunately, is called 'Embarrass the Trainer.' How many of you would like to play 'Embarrass the Trainer?' Oh, oh.

"Here's how it goes: I'm going to leave the room briefly. While I'm out of the room, you'll need to pick something for me to do when I return. In the interest of time, don't make it too complicated. Perhaps you can get me to *turn in circles* [demonstrate] or *take off my shoe* [motion to shoe] or *sit on that table across the room* [point to table]. Maybe you can think of something even more interesting for me to do. Now here's the hard part: When I enter the room, you can't tell me or show me what I'm supposed to do. All you can do is say 'Yes!' Can I hear you say that all together? Ready....*Yes!* Let's try that again, with a bit more energy. Ready....*Yes!* Great! And to get me to the goal faster, at first, say *Yes!* when you see me do anything even remotely like the target behavior. If you're trying to get me to touch my nose, say *Yes!* when I move my hand even slightly toward my nose—just about any movement at first. And you've got to be *quick*, because quick feedback is the best teacher. Let's try it. Watch for me to move my hand toward my nose, and then give me that quick feedback. Are you watching? [Move your hand toward your nose. The group should shout *Yes!* You may need to repeat this until they get the point.] After you've snagged some appropriate behavior in this way, *wait* for a closer approximation to the goal until you say *Yes* again. In other words, wait until my hand goes higher or closer to my nose.

"One more thing, and it's important: There's no saying 'No.' You can't *tell* me what to do, you can't *show* me what to do, and you can't say *No*. Any questions?

"Now I need a volunteer to help the group pick the target behavior after I leave the room." Select a volunteer, and ask the volunteer to bring you back into the room after the group has made its selection.

Leave the room. After a few minutes, the volunteer will retrieve you, and you should allow the group to "shape" your behavior by shouting *Yes!* until the target is reached. This is much easier than it sounds (although see the Comments section below), and it's usually great fun. Stay loose! It's your job at this point to be embarrassed and to show the group how "shaping" works.

Part Two: "Embarrass the Trainee." Trainer (modify as needed): "Good job! But that was only the first half of the exercise. The next part is called 'Embarrass the Trainee.' I like this part much better than the first part. You've seen how the training works. Now I'll need a volunteer to serve as the next guinea pig."

The trainer selects a volunteer—preferably someone outgoing and energetic—and sends him or her out of the room. Then the trainer solicits suggestions for a new target behavior. Ideally, this new target should be a behavior that the volunteer could easily *repeat* several times. So pouring water from a pitcher into a glass is *not* good; whereas, walking around a desk is acceptable.

Once the target behavior is selected, the trainer continues: "When we bring the volunteer into the room, your task will be to 'shape' the behavior we've selected by saying *'Yes!'* in response to increasingly closer approximations to the target. But this time there's a twist. When the target is achieved, get our volunteer to *repeat* the target *three times*, and then *stop saying 'Yes.'* Just *watch* from this point on. Remember, *no more feedback*. This is called an 'extinction' procedure; we've used 'reinforcers' to establish the behavior, and now we're going to withhold them. To help remind you to stop saying *Yes*, keep one eye on me. When I see the target behavior repeated a third time, I'll sit down, like so [demonstrate]. At this point, all we need to do is watch our volunteer for a few minutes.

"What do you think will happen when we shut off the positive feedback? Will our volunteer stop behaving? No, of course not. What *will* the volunteer do? Can you predict?" The trainer can take some suggestions at this point and then continue: "Let's try it and see. Bring in the volunteer!"

The volunteer is brought into the room, and the group shapes and then extinguishes the behavior. The no-feedback period should last from three to five minutes—longer if the performance is especially interesting (see Debriefing section).

When you bring the extinction period to a close, you and the group should offer the volunteer a hearty thanks and congratulations. Failure is frustrating, even for five minutes!

Customizing the Procedure

For Small Groups. No special modifications are needed.

For Large Groups. You may want to appoint a second volunteer to serve as your assistant in Part Two of the exercise. That individual would lead the discussion in which the new target behavior is selected, escort the first volunteer into the room, and shift position to indicate to the group that the extinction period has begun. In this case, it is up to the second volunteer to decide when the target has been achieved and repeated three times. This decision is not especially critical, because the most interesting part of the exercise is the extinction period.

For Non-Business Settings. No special modifications are needed.

For Schools or Homes. No special modifications are needed.

Data Collection

Just about the only way to record this exercise is with videotape equipment. Sometimes the result is so wild that you may want to take the trouble. To obtain general feedback on the exercise, you might want to adapt one of the forms in the Appendix.

FOLLOW-UP

Discussion Questions

1) What did you observe when we stopped saying "Yes"—that is, when we cut off the supply of reinforcers?

2) Did you see any signs of frustration?

3) Did our volunteer repeat the target behavior after the reinforcers stopped?

4) Did the volunteer repeat any of the behaviors we had reinforced on the way to establishing the target?

5) Most important, did the volunteer do any *new* things after we cut off the supply of reinforcers? What new behaviors did you observe?

6) Failure has both positive and negative effects in this exercise. Can you give some examples?

Debriefing

Trainer (modify as needed): "When we cut off the supply of reinforcers, we put our unsuspecting volunteer into the failure mode. No action could produce a *Yes*. What happened? Did the volunteer stop functioning? Not at all. A great deal of behavior occurred—some very significant, given our concern with creativity. Many things happen when behavior is 'extinguished'—that is, when reinforcers are cut off. People get a little upset, as you saw. This is normal and healthy. It happens to great artists and writers and inventors. It's a natural part of the creative process.

"You also see *resurgence*—the recurrence of previously reinforced behaviors. When we're failing, we resort to old methods for rescue. We resort to behaviors that *used to* work in similar situations. In this exercise, the volunteer not only repeats the target behavior a few times, but also some of the earlier forms of that behavior that we reinforced during the shaping process. Resurgence gets many behaviors competing with each other. One result is that feeling of confusion and frustration that we've already talked about. Another is novel behavior. As behaviors compete, they produce new ones—a virtually steady stream. That's a process we want to learn to manipulate to our advantage."

Long-Term Follow-Up

No long-term follow-up is needed; however, it's important to follow-up on the Workplace Challenge in this chapter (Section 5.6).

COMMENTS

Unlike most of the exercises in this volume, this one puts the trainer in an awkward situation: The trainer is at the group's mercy in a shaping exercise. Uh oh. What will they have you do? This is the perfect opportunity for a fun-loving group to get mischievous. Even if your trainees are not out to embarrass you, you may *think* they are during the shaping process. One group decided that they wanted me to turn my head from side to side, but shaping can be tricky. When the group says *Yes*, they'll often strengthen some irrelevant behavior along with the target behavior (the irrelevant behavior is properly called "superstitious" behavior). Whenever I turned my head to the right, I also took a step toward a woman sitting in one corner of the room. The superstitious step got carried along with the head-turn whenever the group said *Yes*. As I got closer to the woman—who also happened to be the director of the facility—I thought to myself, "They want me to kiss this woman! Well, I'm not going to do it!" Fortunately, the group decided that I had done enough head-turning before I had to make the decision.

Shaping occurs quickly. Often a target can be reached in less than a minute. Unfortunately, if the target is met too quickly with the volunteer (in Part Two of the exercise), the extinction may also be rapid and uninteresting. The solution is to select a target behavior that's *moderately* difficult—not too hard and not too easy. Touching one's nose is too easy.

Stacking all the chairs into a large pile is too difficult. The group should do the selecting, but you'll need to guide them.

Other tips: Don't let the group select a target behavior that involves a *sequence* of behaviors. Try to stick with one action. And don't let them pick vocal behavior; stick with movement.

If you've never done this kind of exercise before and you're nervous about letting the group have its way with you, practice first with friends or family. When you're the guinea pig, your best strategy is to move around a lot, trying to elicit a *Yes* as soon as possible.

Finally, what happens if you walk into the room, and the group doesn't say *Yes* to anything you do? This means that the participants haven't quite gotten the idea of "successive approximations." Early on, they need to reinforce almost any behavior and then, rapidly, to increase their requirement. The solution? Simply remind them how shaping works and continue from there.

EXERCISE:
"THE ABCs OF CREATIVITY"

BASICS

Objective

To show that success can interfere with one's ability to solve a simple problem.

Brief Description

The trainer asks some volunteers to spell a series of words using children's alphabet blocks. Some volunteers are given a series of easy tasks before being given a difficult one; others start out with a difficult task.

Materials and Supplies

The main thing you need is a set of standard children's alphabet blocks (or three identical sets if you choose to follow the instructions for large groups). For dramatic effect, you might also want to use a large timer that can be placed in the front of the room; however, a stopwatch or wristwatch will suffice (you'll need three timing devices if you're in the large group mode).

Your volunteers will need to sit, one at a time, at a table or desk in front of the room, so that they face the audience. (You'll need three such tables if you conduct the exercise with three people at once. Ideally, the participants should be spaced well apart, or there should be partitions between them, so that they can't see what the others are doing.)

Time Requirement

Minimum: 30 minutes. Maximum: 1 hour.

PROCEDURE

Basic Procedure

Advance preparation. Before you conduct this exercise, you must prepare the alphabet blocks. The preparation is simple, but you must do it carefully, or the exercise will fail. All you need to do is to *remove all blocks containing the letter "T" (either uppercase or lowercase).* That's easy enough, but when you remove those blocks, you will also be removing other alphabet letters—the ones on the blocks with the *Ts* on them. When you do that, you may need to modify the list of words that you will be asking the first group of volunteers to spell (see below). The participants should be able to spell these words using letters *on the blocks*.

Conducting Part One of the exercise. With the table and chair in place and the blocks out of view, the trainer begins: "We've learned something about the important role that challenge plays in creativity. Let's pursue that a little further, this time with a little spelling contest."

Trainer selects six volunteers, has one sit at the table in front of the room, and sends the other five out of the room. The trainer also selects someone to serve as the Official Timekeeper for the exercise. The timekeeper is stationed at the table in front of the room. The timekeeper should be equipped with a stopwatch or timer and with a bucket of alphabet blocks.

Trainer: "I'm going to ask our volunteer to spell a series of words using children's alphabet blocks, which are in the bucket I gave to our timekeeper. [Show an alphabet block to the group.] On my signal, the timekeeper will dump the blocks in front of our participant, I'll say and spell the word, and the timekeeper will immediately start the clock running. Volunteer: As soon as you've completed spelling the word, say 'Done!' and raise your hand, so the timekeeper can stop the clock and record your time. Ready? Timekeeper, please dump the blocks. Volunteer, Please spell BOX—that's BOX—as quickly as possible. Go!"

As soon as the volunteer has located the correct alphabet letters and arranged them in order (this should only take a few seconds), you should congratulate the volunteer, and the timekeeper should announce the time and record it on the chart you've provided (see Form 5.3.1).

This procedure should be repeated for the words ZIP, MAN, HOP, and LIT.

The volunteer should have no trouble with the first four words (BOX, ZIP, MAN, and HOP) but may have some difficulty with LIT, because the blocks do not contain any Ts. The solution is simple, of course—if you're a child! You simply use any blocks to form the *shape* of a T, or perhaps the shapes of all three letters (L, I, and T). In any case, the solution time for LIT will probably be longer than for the first four words. If the volunteer gets frustrated, say, "I'm sorry, but all I can do is repeat the instructions I've already given you: Your task is to use these blocks to spell the word LIT." If necessary, add "It can be done. You can do it." If time is short, after five minutes have elapsed you may want to start giving the volunteer some hints; ideally, you'll just keep waiting. When the first volunteer has finished, this entire procedure should be repeated for each of the next two volunteers.

Conducting Part Two of the exercise. Now the fourth, fifth, and sixth volunteers should be given their chance; however, they will be asked to spell just one word: LIT. The instructions from Part One of the exercise should be modified accordingly.

When all six of the volunteers have completed the task, the timekeeper needs to compute only two numbers: the average time it took the first group (of three volunteers) to spell LIT, and the average time it took the second group to spell LIT (Form 5.3.1).

Typically, the average time is much longer in the first group than in the second: Previous success at solving the problem a certain way interferes with creativity when the problem changes.

Customizing the Procedure

For Small Groups. In the directions given above, six volunteers are used (three in each condition) in order to yield group averages. The point of averaging is to reduce the impact of spurious outlying values. If you're working with a small group, you may not have this luxury, in which case you may be able to employ only one or two individuals in each condition.

For Large Groups. If resources permit, you may want to set up a kind of three-ring circus: Set up three tables in front of the auditorium, appoint three timekeepers, and have three volunteers compete at the same time. With a real-time competition, the exercise will be more fun, and the outcome will be more dramatic.

For Non-Business Settings. No special modifications are needed.

For Schools or Homes. Children will have to know how to read and spell the simple words used in this exercise in order to complete it. Familiarity with alphabet blocks isn't enough!

Other Options

Change the words to suit your needs (and your particular brand of alphabet blocks), but do so cautiously: It's important that all the words be the same length, and all the words except the test word should be easy to spell using the alphabet letters printed on the blocks.

Data Collection

Form 5.3.1 will allow you or the timekeeper to record the essential data. Because the groups are so small, the arithmetic mean (the "average") may be misleading, so you may want to use the medians instead. If you want your results to have scientific validity, simply pool them across different training sessions. This will give you a larger group size, which will help you control for outlying points.

FOLLOW-UP

Discussion Questions

1) Was everyone able to spell LIT? Did some people have more trouble than others? Who had trouble, and why?
2) What difference, if any, did a "history of success" make? Did experience on the simple spelling tasks help or hurt on the more difficult task?
3) What extinction effects did you observe when the participants were asked to spell LIT?
4) Previous success can both help and hurt when you're faced with a new problem. Can you think of examples?

Debriefing

Trainer (modify as needed): "Our valiant volunteers were given a very simple problem to solve: Spell the word LIT using some alphabet blocks. We discovered that this task could become much harder if people had had success in using the blocks a certain way. If they had learned to pay attention to the letters on the face of the blocks, they had some difficulty paying attention to other properties of the blocks. If they had learned to spell words using the printed letters, they had some trouble spelling words using the shapes of the blocks.

"Generativity Theory can help us to understand what's happening here. Failure helps spur the creative process by getting many old behaviors to compete. But if we've had too much success in some context, certain behaviors will be very strong in that context. We'll rely on them for a very long time, and the extinction process will be slowed down. In other words, if we've been too successful in some situation, we'll be insensitive to changing conditions. Is this relevant to our businesses or even our personal lives? How so? And what's the solution to this dilemma? Should we live our lives on the brink of failure? Should we seek more challenges?"

Long-Term Follow-Up

This exercise sometimes has an enormous impact on trainees. As part of a thirty-day follow-up, you may want to ask whether participants remember the exercise, whether they have benefited from it personally, and whether they have applied it to the workplace. You can explore these issues more formally as part of the follow-up for the Workplace Challenge (Section 5.6).

COMMENTS

If you've never tried this exercise before, practice on colleagues and friends before you put yourself on the firing line with your trainees. Like most procedures, it's simple when you know how to do it, but trivial factors can cause problems. For example, some alphabet blocks contain pictures or diagrams that resemble alphabet letters. You may find that your participant will insist that a rotated candlestick or sailboat makes a perfectly good T. If you want to avoid such problems, test out your blocks, and eliminate the offending ones.

As usual, some people may show signs of frustration when they can't find the letter T. Remember that in the context of these games, frustration is a *good* sign, not a bad one. Reminding the group that that's the case will relieve some of the pressure, and, if necessary, encourage the volunteer by saying, "You can do it." As noted earlier, you can also repeat the original instructions: "Use the blocks to spell the word LIT." That often serves as a powerful spur toward the solution, because it reminds people that you never put any restriction on *how* the blocks were to be used. They imposed the restriction themselves, and their success in using the printed letters to spell earlier words didn't help when the requirements of the problem changed.

Scoring Sheet
Exercise: "The ABCs of Creativity"

Date:_____ Organization:_____ Trainer:_____

Is there a time limit? Yes ☐   No ☐   If so, what is it? _____ minutes.

Part One

SOLUTION TIMES

Word	Participant 1	2	3	Mean	Median
1-				XXXXXX	XXXXXX
2-				XXXXXX	XXXXXX
3-				XXXXXX	XXXXXX
4-				XXXXXX	XXXXXX
5*-					

*Record "N.S." if there is no solution in the allotted time.

Part Two

SOLUTION TIMES

Word	Participant 1	2	3	Mean	Median
5-					

To share data or comments with the author, fax this form to 619-436-4490.

From *Creativity Games for Trainers*, by Dr. Robert Epstein. E-mail address: repstein@rohan.sdsu.edu.

EXERCISE: "THE ULTIMATE CHALLENGE GAME"

BASICS

Objective

To teach participants the value that open-ended problems have in spurring creativity.

Brief Description

Participants are asked to solve ultimate, open-ended problems that have no solutions.

Materials and Supplies

Form 5.4.1 can be copied for all participants, or blank paper can be used instead.

Time Requirement

Minimum: 20 minutes. Maximum: 60 minutes.

PROCEDURE

Basic Procedure

Trainer (modify as needed): "This next exercise is very easy—or very difficult. It just depends on how you look at it. We've seen that failure helps promote creativity because it gets 'multiple repertoires of behavior' competing. We've even seen that too much success can impair the creative process by slowing down this competition. But how can we put failure to work for us? And how can we get people to fail without getting them to quit? The answer is to establish one or more Controlled Failure Systems, one of which we're about to explore.

"This exercise is truly very simple, just like our Daydream exercise [Section 2.2]. Get a paper and pencil ready. I'm going to give you three minutes to solve a problem. You may not come up with the perfect answer in that time, but it's important that you write down at least one answer—even if it seems a little silly. After the three minutes are up, I'll ask several of you to share your answers with the group. Any questions?

"Here is your first problem: *Propose a way to eliminate all air pollution in this country within the next thirty days*. You have three minutes. Go."

When three minutes have passed, call on some members of the group to share their ideas. As time permits, pose some additional questions, such as:

> *Tell us how to build a machine that will allow people to travel in time.*

> *Propose a way to send someone to the moon for the price of a subway token.*

> *Mt. Everest is blocking your view. Propose a scheme for knocking it down.*

> *You need to raise a billion dollars by tomorrow at noon. Tell us how you're going to do it.*

Add some ultimate questions that are relevant to your business, or ask the group to propose some questions of this sort. If you work for the telephone company, ask, "What will the perfect telephone be like one hundred years from now?" Again, give participants three minutes to answer, and then discuss some of the answers.

Customizing the Procedure

For Small Groups. In a small group, everyone's answers can be shared.

For Large Groups. In a large group, people often try to lose themselves in the crowd. One way to combat this is to announce that after the answers are written, everyone will need to trade papers with someone else. The recipients will be the ones to raise their hands and share the ideas of their associates.

For Non-Business Settings. The problems should suit the audience. For example, if you're working with the staff of a marine park (a marvelous experience, by the way, which I had the pleasure of doing a few years ago), ask, "You have thirty days in which to end all water pollution on this planet. How do you do it?" or "How can we get the marine creatures in this park to take care of themselves, so we can all stay home?"

For Schools or Homes. Again, the problems should be suitable to the group. Other than that, no special modifications are needed.

Other Options

You may want to use an overhead projector or other display device to project the questions onto a screen, especially when you're working in a large space. You may also want to consider giving participants a longer time to work on a particular problem. There's nothing sacred about the three-minute requirement.

Data Collection

Form 5.4.1 (or a variant) will allow you to collect examples of the solutions you receive to open-ended problems.

FOLLOW-UP

Discussion Questions

1) When faced with difficult questions, do people simply shut down? What does happen? How do people react?

2) What kinds of replies do people give? Are the replies entirely useless?

3) How do ultimate questions spur creativity? What is the underlying mechanism?

4) What are the ultimate challenges in our industry?

5) Could ultimate challenges be used by our company on a regular basis to develop new ideas? How so?

Debriefing

Trainer (modify as needed): "Ultimate challenges spur creativity in two ways: First, because the problems are impossible to solve, they generate multiple repertoires of behavior—one of the extinction phenomena that we discussed earlier. Second, they spur new ideas that are at least *pertinent* to the ultimate challenge. Ultimate challenges *direct* the creative process toward useful goals.

"What if a few minutes were set aside each week during which everyone in your organization was faced with an ultimate challenge for your industry? Would that practice yield any useful ideas?

"The Ultimate Challenge is an example of a Controlled Failure System—a system that gives people permission to fail as a means of promoting creativity. Ultimate Challenges are helpful because failure produces 'resurgence,' and that gets multiple repertoires going."

The trainer may also want to remind participants of any useful or interesting ideas that were generated during the exercise.

Long-Term Follow-Up

If some interesting ideas have turned up during the training session, you may want to track them. You may also want to determine whether any of the participants tried to implement an Ultimate Challenge procedure.

COMMENTS

The key to success in this game is in reminding participants to write down *at least one answer* to every question posed. People always have answers, but they are often reluctant to share them. Socialization has its advantages, but it also has costs—especially when creativity is on the line.

Participant's Notes and Evaluation
Exercise: "The Ultimate Challenge Game"

CHALLENGES	SOLUTIONS

"The Ultimate Challenge Game" (Continued)

Participant's name and contact information (optional):

_____

_____

_____

_____

Organization:

_____

_____

Position:

_____

_____

Date:

_____

_____

Trainer:

_____

_____

Value of the exercise:

LOW   ☐   ☐   ☐   ☐   ☐   HIGH

Suggestions for improving the exercise:

_____

_____

_____

_____

_____

To share data or comments with the author, fax this form to 619-436-4490.

*From **Creativity Games for Trainers**, by Dr. Robert Epstein. E-mail address: repstein@rohan.sdsu.edu.*

EXERCISE:
DESIGN CHALLENGE

BASICS

Objective

To further convince participants of the value that failure has in promoting creativity by having the participants themselves design an exercise that makes this point.

Brief Description

Participants are asked to spend a few minutes designing another exercise along the lines of the previous exercises in this chapter. They then carry out the new exercise. They may require the trainer to participate.

Materials and Supplies

They may use (a) any of the materials and supplies from the previous exercises in this chapter and (b) any additional materials, objects, or supplies that are present in the room.

Time Requirement

Minimum: 45 minutes. Maximum: 90 minutes.

PROCEDURE

Basic Procedure

Trainer (modify as needed): "In the exercises we've just completed, we've seen that failure ('extinction') can play an important role in creativity, because one effect of failure is to get multiple repertoires of behavior to compete. Now comes the next step: to turn this very process in on itself. In this next exercise, your challenge is to design a new exercise that demonstrates the role that challenge plays in creativity. Your challenge is to teach us more about challenge. You'll have ten minutes in which to design this new task. Here are some guidelines: (a) you can make use of any of the objects and materials that we've used in previous exercises (in this section or prior sections); (b) you can make use of any other objects or materials in this room; (c) you can assign people to different roles and send people out of the room, as necessary; (d) you can use me as one of the participants in this new exercise. After the ten-minute design period is over, you'll have an additional twenty minutes in which to conduct the exercise. After that, a representative from your group will lead us all in a short debriefing to evaluate the outcome of the new exercise and to see whether your goals have been met."

Customizing the Procedure

For Small Groups. Small groups can be broken up into teams of approximately five people each. Each team should design its own exercise. If time allows, each team should be allowed to conduct the exercise it has designed, using the trainer and the other teams as participants.

For Large Groups. In a large auditorium where time is limited, a single team should be assembled, and that group should design an exercise for the rest of the audience. The team may need to leave the room to design the exercise. Alternatively, the larger group can be given a break while the team creates its design.

For Non-Business Settings. No special modifications are needed.

For Schools or Homes. As with previous Design Challenges, the trainer or teacher should lead the children in the design of the new exercise, eliciting suggestions and comments from them. With young children, the trainer should have a new exercise in mind before eliciting any feedback.

Other Options

As noted earlier, trainers should feel free to experiment with the way they conduct all Design Challenge exercises.

It's not necessary to complete all three of the exercises in this section before beginning the Design Challenge, but at least one and preferably two others should be completed first.

The time requirements may need to be changed: The group may need more than ten minutes for design, and the new exercise may take longer than twenty minutes to conduct.

Data Collection

The trainer may wish to use or modify Form A.3 in the Appendix of this book (p. 261).

FOLLOW-UP

Discussion Questions

1) What was the goal of this exercise? Did we reach that goal? Why or why not?
2) How could this exercise be improved?

3) What did this exercise teach us, if anything?

4) How can we relate the outcome of this exercise to the outcomes of the previous exercises in this chapter?

5) Does failure have value? Have your views on this issue changed at all since we began this series of exercises?

Debriefing

Trainer (modify as appropriate): "This last exercise—a challenge about challenge—has, I hope, taken us to a new level in our understanding of the creative process. To design it, you profited from the very process that we've been learning about in this section. You accepted a challenge in order to learn more about the effect that challenge has on creativity. Our next exercise will allow us to focus more directly on the organization itself."

Long-Term Follow-Up

This exercise does not require a long-term follow-up. If, however, there has been a dramatic result—a surprising or significant example of creativity, for example—that result should be preserved and posted so people will remember it and refer back to it. The point is to remind people how much creativity is valued in the organization.

COMMENTS

As always, trainers need to ensure: (a) that everyone gets a chance to participate, (b) that the exercise is fun and upbeat, and (c) that time limits are respected. A group-designed exercise may overlook these requirements, so the trainer may need to intervene. If several exercises are to be conducted, the trainer will need to schedule breaks.

EXERCISE:
WORKPLACE CHALLENGE

BASICS

Objective

To extend the lessons of the previous exercises in this chapter to specific organizational settings.

Brief Description

Participants are asked to design an application, procedure, or policy (a) that is based on principles, methods, or outcomes from previous exercises in this chapter and (b) that has specific benefits for their particular workplaces.

Required Materials and Supplies

Writing materials.

Optional Materials and Supplies

Large, blank sheets of paper (without lines) should be available to encourage people to make diagrams or drawings. Word processors may be helpful in some settings.

Time Requirement

Minimum: 20 minutes. Maximum: 1 hour.

PROCEDURE

Basic Procedure

Trainer (modify as appropriate): "Our next step is to try to extend what we've learned to our particular organizational setting. If failure spurs creativity—and if too much success can interfere with creativity—how can we improve our workplace to take advantage of these facts? What policies or procedures might we change? How might we improve the work environment? How might we change or improve our training procedures? What other changes might we make? What outcomes—positive and negative—might we expect to result from such changes?

"Let's take ten minutes to sketch out our ideas. As usual, don't be overly concerned just yet about the practicality of your suggestions. Don't think too much about budget. Just think, 'How might my organization be improved to take advantage of the fact that *failure* has value in promoting creativity?' After ten minutes have passed, I'll ask some of you to share your ideas with the group, and we'll discuss them together. Any questions?"

When the design period is over, the trainer should review some of the proposals with the group.

Customizing the Procedure

For Small Groups. In a small group, everyone should be given an opportunity to present his or her ideas. The trainer should emphasize the value of every idea, no matter how impractical. *After* all of the ideas have been presented, the group can begin the task of assessing their feasibility and value.

For Large Groups. In a large group, everyone can sketch out ideas on paper, but the trainer will be able to call on only a few people to present them to the group.

For Non-Business Settings. No special modifications are needed.

For Schools or Homes. Children may need close supervision by the trainer or teacher.

Other Options

Participants should be allowed to work together in small groups (although see the caveats in Chapter 8 of this volume). Where an audience includes members of different organizations, the trainer should make sure that each organization is given some consideration.

The ten-minute period is just a suggestion. A shorter or longer period may be more appropriate for your group.

Data Collection

Trainers may wish to use or modify Form A.1 in the Appendix of this volume (p. 261).

FOLLOW-UP

Discussion Questions

1) How is failure dealt with in your organization? Does this approach enhance or inhibit creativity?

2) Do Controlled Failure Systems currently exist in your organization? If so, please describe them. How could they be improved?

3) What's the down side of failure? How can you protect against it?
4) Would it be feasible to introduce any Controlled Failure Systems to your organization?

Debriefing

Trainer (modify as appropriate): "We've taken a step toward applying what we've learned about failure to our organization. Too much of anything is a bad thing, so people say. And too much failure would also be a disaster, both for us as individuals and for our organization. As we've seen, not enough failure can also be problematic. It can make us complacent, make us unable to deal with the demands of a changing world or marketplace."

Long-Term Follow-Up

Workplace Challenges should, whenever possible, be followed up. The trainer should encourage participants to complete and return Form A.2 (or some equivalent) in the Appendix of this volume (p. 261) thirty days after the completion of training. If possible, trainers should contact participants who don't return the forms on their own. A brief telephone interview will allow trainers to complete the form. Trainers should use the replies to evaluate and improve their own training procedures. The replies will also furnish examples of successes and failures that can be used in future training. Participants who expect some form of follow-up are more likely to implement material that they have mastered in training. Without follow-up, training often has little more than entertainment value.

COMMENTS

The Workplace Challenge is an essential tool for allowing participants to connect relatively abstract exercises with the real world. Proposals will necessarily be tentative, and they may not be practical. At this point, it's the effort that counts.

CHALLENGING:
GENERAL DEBRIEFING

It's natural to fear failure. No one should be ashamed of such fear. But it's important that we recognize the value of failure, as well. As managers, trainers, teachers, and parents—people responsible for the behavior of others—it's especially important that we teach people the value of failure, that we encourage people to take risks from time to time, and that we challenge our trainees with difficult problems.

Here are some of the major concepts we explored in the exercises in this section:

- In the "Not-for-the-Fainthearted Game" we saw that when reinforcement is discontinued, people keep behaving. They get a little frustrated, they repeat what they've learned, and then they try new approaches. The extinction process accelerates creativity. *Waiting*—giving the generative process the time to work—can have tremendous value.

- In the "ABCs" game we saw that if you have great success solving a problem a certain way, you may have trouble abandoning that approach when the circumstances demand a new one. Too much success can interfere with creativity.

- In the "Ultimate Challenge" exercise, we saw that difficult, open-ended problems can be powerful spurs to creativity.

- In our Workplace Challenge, we attempted to design Controlled Failure Systems that will tap creativity without causing undue stress.

Life without challenge is boring. Business without challenge is temporary.

CHAPTER 6

"BROADENING" GAMES:
CAN LEARNING MAKE US
MORE CREATIVE?

BROADENING:
ORIENTATION

For repertoires of behavior to participate in a creative mix, they must first exist. You can't solve a problem in quantum mechanics if you think quantum mechanics has something to do with fixing a small car. Training is essential to creativity, because training provides more repertoires for the mix.

Broadening—the deliberate establishment of new and diverse repertoires of behavior—is a powerful way to enhance creativity, and it's probably the best way of *directing* creativity toward specific ends.

Many great leaps in entrepreneurship, invention, and the arts come from people who bring diverse backgrounds to their fields. If your goal is to boost creativity in your organization, you have two ways to change the training backgrounds of your employees: Either provide some new training, or hire some new employees!

In the exercises that follow, we'll explore what happens to creativity when our knowledge and skills are limited, and we'll compare what happens when our knowledge and skills are broad.

In "The News-You-Can-Use Game," we'll train some people well and others less well, and then we'll compare the performances when our trainees are faced with a problem. In "The Broader-the-Better Game," we'll ask people to create when looking at a problem narrowly, and then we'll ask them to create when looking at a problem broadly. Finally, in the Design and Workplace Challenges, participants will be given an opportunity to apply what they've learned.

EXERCISE: "THE NEWS-YOU-CAN-USE GAME"

BASICS

Objective

To demonstrate that previous learning has an impact on the creative process.

Brief Description

Volunteers are given some information about newspapers and then asked to solve a simple problem using a newspaper.

Materials and Supplies

Newspapers! One full-size daily is probably sufficient, unless you plan to have everyone participate (see the Small Groups option, below). You'll also need a small round balloon (or another very light object) and a roll of tape. A long table in the front of the room would be helpful but isn't necessary. An overhead projector and screen would also be helpful. You can also conduct this exercise as a *gedunken* exercise (a thinking exercise) without any objects at all (see Other Options), but doing the exercise with the objects will probably have more of an impact on your trainees.

Time Requirement

Minimum: 30 minutes. Maximum: 1 hour.

PROCEDURE

Basic Procedure

Select two volunteers and have them leave the room. Then inflate a balloon and place it at one end of the long table, so that it's too far away to reach from the other end of the table. If you prefer, you can place a line on the floor with a piece of masking tape and then place the balloon on the floor about six feet away from the line. Almost any arrangement will do, as long as the balloon is out of reach by two or three feet. Place the newspaper and roll of tape at the near end of table (far from the balloon) or wherever it is that the volunteer is going to stand.

For dramatic effect, you may want to grab a marker at this point and label the balloon "BONUS" or "PROMOTION" or "BALLOON PAYMENT" or something along those lines.

Trainer (modify as needed): "Training—previous experience—makes a difference in creativity, because training helps to determine the set of behaviors that's available to produce new ones. In this exercise—'The News-You-Can-Use Game'—I'm going to give each of our volunteers some different training and them ask them to solve a simple problem."

Appoint a timekeeper, and instruct the timekeeper to time the performance of each volunteer from the time you say "Begin" until the performance is completed. Then bring in the first volunteer.

Trainer: "I'm going to ask you to solve a simple problem, but first I'm going to provide some training. Here is the information."

Project Form 6.2.1 (or equivalent) onto the screen, and read the text aloud. Then continue, "Now here is the problem: Please stand on this spot [show volunteer the spot] and, using this newspaper and tape, retrieve the balloon as quickly as possible. You have five minutes. You may not use any other objects; you may not move out of this position; and you may not ask others for help. Begin."

When the participant has finished the task (or the maximum time has been reached), repeat this procedure with the second volunteer, this time using Form 6.2.2.

The two forms differ in only one significant respect: Form 6.2.2 includes instructions for rolling up a newspaper to make a fishing rod. The first volunteer may or may not know how to construct such a device; the second volunteer definitely has this information and thus should have an easier time solving the problem.

The solution to the problem (or at least the one I have in mind!) is as follows: Roll up the newspaper tightly into a long rod (perhaps using the tape secure it). Attach a piece of tape to the end of the rod so that a sticky surface is exposed. Extend the rod toward the balloon, touch the sticky surface to it, and retrieve the balloon.

Your discussion should focus on the differences between the two performances. If the differences were minimal, or if the result was opposite from the expected one, your discussion should focus on explaining the outcome.

Customizing the Procedure

For Small Groups. You can add a step to the procedure when the group is small. After you send out the volunteers, distribute Form 6.2.1 to half the group and Form 6.2.2 to the other half. Have everyone read the instructions, and then ask them to solve the problem on paper. Find out how many people in each of the two sub-groups solved the problem, and briefly explore the effect of the brief "training." Then bring in the volunteers and proceed as above.

For Large Groups. In a large auditorium, you may want to arrange for video projection to allow the audience a clearer picture of what the volunteers are doing.

For Non-Business Settings. The balloon should be labeled in a manner appropriate to the setting, and you might want to alter the text in Forms 6.2.1 and 6.2.2. No other special modifications are needed.

For Schools or Homes. Even with the "fishing rod" instructions, children will have great difficulty solving the balloon problem. The solution involves a number of components, for one thing, and most of them are unfamiliar to children: rolling a newspaper, attaching tape to newspaper with the sticky side exposed, using tape to catch and pull an object, and so on. Rolling the newspaper might involve fine-motor skills that the child has not yet mastered. You may want to simplify the problem accordingly.

Other Options

As I noted earlier, you can conduct this entire exercise as a *gedunken* exercise, without any props. Paper and pencil will do. The two types of instructions can be distributed on paper, one to each half of the group.

If you're using a balloon, you can add spice (and noise) to the proceedings by changing the goal: Instead of instructing the volunteers to retrieve the balloon, tell them that their mission is to pop it. (They'll need to retrieve it first.)

If it's inconvenient for you to project the instructions onto a screen, you can simply read them aloud.

Data Collection

Forms 6.2.1 and 6.2.2 can be used to collect data. The volunteers' performances can best be captured on videotape.

FOLLOW-UP

Discussion Questions

1) What was the difference in the two types of "training" the volunteers received?
2) Did different training produce different outcomes? Why or why not?
3) Why does previous learning affect creativity?
4) How can you direct creativity toward useful ends by providing certain training?

Debriefing

Trainer (modify as needed): "We've seen that training makes a difference in creativity. Generative processes always take us beyond what we already know, but only so far. If we lack certain training or knowledge that's critical to solving a particular problem, we may never solve it. Can we know for sure what training is required for every new situation? No, we cannot. But a good rule of thumb is that *the more training people have had and the more diverse that training, the more creative they will be.*"

Long-Term Follow-Up

As always, if some remarkable behavior turns up during this exercise, take note of it and post it for all to see. Make it known that your organization *values* creativity.

COMMENTS

What if the volunteer who has been taught to make a fishing rod fails to solve the problem? What if that volunteer takes longer to solve the problem than the volunteer who has not received these instructions? With a group size of two (groups don't get any smaller!), such unlikely outcomes are *bound* to happen sometimes. You'll get the "wrong" result for simple reasons: The first volunteer has already had extensive experience rolling up newspapers (perhaps to swat flies); the second volunteer may have misunderstood your instructions; the first volunteer may be relaxed in front of groups, while the second volunteer might be a nervous wreck. If the worst happens, don't worry about it. State what *usually* happens and then spend a few minutes having the group help you figure out why you got a different result today. Remember: "In every crisis, there's an opportunity."

If you use the two-step procedure (see the Small Groups section, above), your group results will be more reliable than the results you get with the volunteers.

Training Guide
Exercise: "The News-You-Can-Use Game"

Here are ten possible uses for a newspaper. Please study them carefully.

1) You can read it and learn about news, entertainment, and bargains.

2) You can cover your head with it during a sudden rainstorm.

3) You can line your bird cage with it.

4) You can tear it into strips and use it to start your camp fire.

5) You can wad it and use it as packing material.

6) You can stuff it into a hole to block a draft.

7) You can stack newspapers and then climb onto the stack to extend your reach.

8) You can use it as a pad to sit on.

9) You can fold it into a hat that looks like Napoleon's.

10) You can line your kitchen shelves with it.

Below, please sketch the solution to the problem that the trainer will give you:

*To share data or comments with the
author, fax this form to 619-436-4490.*   *From **Creativity Games for Trainers**, by Dr. Robert
Epstein. E-mail address: repstein@rohan.sdsu.edu.*

"The News-You-Can-Use Game" *(Continued)*

Participant's name and contact information (optional):

_____
_____
_____
_____

Organization:

_____
_____

Position:

_____
_____

Date:

_____
_____

Trainer:

_____
_____

Value of the exercise:

LOW ☐ ☐ ☐ ☐ ☐ HIGH

Suggestions for improving the exercise:

_____
_____
_____
_____
_____

To share data or comments with the author, fax this form to 619-436-4490.

*From **Creativity Games for Trainers**, by Dr. Robert Epstein. E-mail address: repstein@rohan.sdsu.edu.*

Training Guide
Exercise: "The News-You-Can-Use Game"

Here are ten possible uses for a newspaper. Please study them carefully.

1) You can read it and learn about news, entertainment, and bargains.

2) You can cover your head with it during a sudden rainstorm.

3) You can line your bird cage with it.

4) You can tear it into strips and use it to start your camp fire.

5) You can wad it and use it as packing material.

6) You can stuff it into a hole to block a draft.

7) You can stack newspapers and then climb onto the stack to extend your reach.

8) You can roll a page of it up tightly to make a fishing pole.

9) You can fold it into a hat that looks like Napoleon's.

10) You can line your kitchen shelves with it.

Below, please sketch the solution to the problem that the trainer will give you:

To share data or comments with the
author, fax this form to 619-436-4490.

*From **Creativity Games for Trainers**, by Dr. Robert*
Epstein. E-mail address: repstein@rohan.sdsu.edu.

"The News-You-Can-Use Game" (Continued)

Participant's name and contact information (optional):

_____

_____

_____

_____

Organization:

_____

_____

Position:

_____

_____

Date:

_____

_____

Trainer:

_____

_____

Value of the exercise:

_____

LOW   ☐   ☐   ☐   ☐   ☐   HIGH

Suggestions for improving the exercise:

_____

_____

_____

_____

_____

_____

*To share data or comments with the
author, fax this form to 619-436-4490.*

*From **Creativity Games for Trainers**, by Dr. Robert
Epstein. E-mail address: repstein@rohan.sdsu.edu.*

EXERCISE: "THE-BROADER-THE-BETTER GAME"

BASICS

Objective

To demonstrate that you usually get more and better ideas when you bring diverse skills to bear on solving a problem.

Brief Description

Participants generate two lists of activities—one that's pertinent to their own organization (like "Marketing" or "Management") and the other that's pertinent to the non-business world (like "Bowling" or "Mowing the Lawn"). In Part One of the exercise, participants devise new products or services based on their knowledge of an activity in the first list; in Part Two, participants generate new products or services based on their knowledge of an activity in each of the two lists.

Materials and Supplies

You'll need a blackboard or flipchart. You may also want to distribute copies of Form 6.3.1 to all participants.

Time Requirement

Minimum: 30 minutes. Maximum: 1 hour.

PROCEDURE

Basic Procedure

Part One. Trainer (modify as needed): "Let's try using our expertise to develop a new product or service. We're going to do this in two different ways. To start, I'll need you to help me create a list of activities that currently exist in your organization. These can be the names of departments or divisions (like 'Marketing' or 'Sales') or the names of more specific activities (like 'photocopying' or 'shipping'). Please give me activities that you know a lot about. Suggestions?"

Based on suggestions from the group, make a list of between ten and twenty activities on the blackboard or flipchart.

Continue as follows: "Now I'd like each of you to focus on just *one* of these activities. Based on what you know about it, take a few minutes to try to develop a new product or service—one with possible market value. For example, say you know that it's frustrating waiting in line to use the photocopy machine. Perhaps you can devise a way for people to be entertained while they're waiting—or, better yet, a way for people to get work done. Think about what you know about *that activity only*. Try not to stray too far outside the photocopy room to design your new product or service. Questions?"

Allow people a few minutes to jot down their ideas, and then call on people to hear some of their suggestions.

Part Two. Trainer (modify as needed). "Now let's make a new list—this time, a list of activities that you know about *outside* the organization—things like 'singing,' 'mowing the lawn,' or 'bowling.' Suggestions?"

Based on suggestions from the group, make a new list of between ten and twenty activities. Once again, be sure these are activities in which your participants have expertise.

Trainer: "Now let's try developing that new product or service again. This time, use your expertise in *two* areas—the organizational activity (preferably, the one you used a few minutes ago) and one of the *outside* activities. So now, perhaps, you're in the photocopy room again, and this time you're also thinking about your special expertise in singing. Perhaps you envision a photocopy machine with a built-in stereo or a built-in kareoke screen. Perhaps you make a slight leap from that to a photocopy machine with a running display or today's news or stock market results. Any questions?"

Again, allow a few minutes for people to jot down their ideas, and then call on some of them to report on their new products or services.

Customizing the Procedure

For Small Groups. No special modifications are needed.

For Large Groups. No special modifications are needed, although a display screen would be helpful in a large auditorium. Markers, a blank sheet of acetate, and an overhead projector will serve.

For Non-Business Settings. For a non-business group, you'll need to modify the instructions to accommodate the activities that are specific to the group. For virtually any group, the basic idea is the same, however. You construct two separate lists, one specific to professional activities and the other specific to non-professional activities.

For Schools or Homes. Suitably modified, this game can easily be conducted with children. The key is to make use of what the children know. Here is the basic idea: "Let's invent something that will help us do our homework. How can we do this using things in this room? What else do we know a lot about? Could we take ideas from that, too?"

Other Options

If time allows, you can expand the problem to include two or more outside activities. With more ideas available, you'll probably get more interesting solutions. Unfortunately, you'll also get more confusion, and it will take more time to sort things out. If you don't have the time, stick with the original instructions. (See Chapter 7 on "Surrounding," as well as Section 9.2, for further information.)

Data Collection

Form 6.3.1 can be used to help you capture some of your participants' ideas.

FOLLOW-UP

Discussion Questions

1) What kinds of products or services did you develop when you were restricted to thinking about one activity?

2) When you began to think about an outside activity, what effect did that have on your thinking? Did you feel confused?

3) What kinds of products or services did you develop when you were thinking about two unrelated activities?

4) Did it help or hurt to think about two topics at once? How so?

5) If you have problems to solve, are you better off with narrow or diverse training? Why?

6) How could the results of this exercise be applied to your workplace?

7) How could training in different subject areas be used to direct the creative process?

Debriefing

Trainer (modify as needed): "We've cheated a bit in this exercise. In a full-blown demonstration of the importance of 'broadening,' we'd have to train you in various ways and then look at the effect such training has on creativity. With luck, we'd find that broader or more diverse training would make you better able to solve a variety of problems. That's what laboratory studies of creativity show. In a hands-on training session, we can't do that. We have to make do with what you've already learned. By dividing up what you know into lists, we could pretend at first that your skills were very limited, and then we could pretend that we were giving you some new skills.

"When you tried to invent a new product or service in the first part of the exercise, we deliberately limited your abilities. How well did you do? In Part Two of the exercise, we expanded your abilities. How did that go?

"Generally, the more skills—and the more diverse the skills—that you bring to a problem, the more creative you will be. You may also need more time to work out a solution, especially if you bring a great wealth of information to the task. With many repertoires competing, you may also feel more confused. But that's a good sign, not a bad one."

Long-Term Follow-Up

At a thirty-day follow-up, you may find it interesting to learn whether any of the participants actually implemented any of the ideas that were generated during the exercise. Has the photocopy room become more user-friendly?

COMMENTS

You may not get "better" ideas in Part Two of this exercise, but you should get a great many ideas that are clearly born of two different domains. That should give you the ammunition you need to drive home the key points: (1) Diverse training leads to very different—and probably more interesting—thinking than narrow training does. (2) Training can be used deliberately to influence the creative process.

Participant's Notes and Evaluation
Exercise: "The-Broader-the-Better Game"

PART ONE: Please sketch or describe a new product or service.

PART TWO: Please sketch or describe a new product or service.

To share data or comments with the author, fax this form to 619-436-4490.

*From **Creativity Games for Trainers**, by Dr. Robert Epstein. E-mail address: repstein@rohan.sdsu.edu.*

"The-Broader-the-Better Game" (Continued)

Participant's name and contact information (optional):

_____

_____

_____

_____

Organization:

_____

_____

Position:

_____

_____

Date:

_____

_____

Trainer:

_____

_____

Value of the exercise:

LOW   ☐   ☐   ☐   ☐   ☐   HIGH

Suggestions for improving the exercise:

_____

_____

_____

_____

_____

_____

EXERCISE:
DESIGN CHALLENGE

BASICS

Objective

To further demonstrate the importance of diverse training in creativity, in this case, by having the participants themselves design an exercise that makes this point.

Brief Description

Participants are asked to spend a few minutes designing another exercise along the lines of the previous exercises in this chapter. They then carry out the new exercise. They may require the trainer to participate.

Materials and Supplies

They may use (a) any of the materials and supplies from the previous exercises in this chapter and (b) any additional materials, objects, or supplies that are present in the room.

Time Requirement

Minimum: 30 minutes. Maximum: 90 minutes.

PROCEDURE

Basic Procedure

Trainer: "In the exercises we've just completed, we've seen that diverse training facilitates the creative process. Now comes the next step: to use your creative energies to design an exercise that further demonstrates the point. You'll have ten minutes in which to design this new task. Here are some guidelines: (a) you can make use of any of the objects and materials that we've used in previous exercises; (b) you can make use of any other objects or materials in this room; (c) you can assign people to different roles and send people out of the room, as necessary; (d) you can use me as one of the participants in this new exercise. After the ten-minute design period is over, you'll have an additional ten minutes in which to conduct the exercise. After that, a representative from the group will lead us all in a short debriefing to evaluate the outcome of the new exercise and to see whether your goals have been met."

Customizing the Procedure

For Small Groups. Small groups can be broken up into teams of approximately five people each. Each team should design its own exercise. If time allows, each team should be allowed to conduct the exercise it has designed, using the trainer and the other teams as participants.

For Large Groups. In a large auditorium where time is limited, a single team should be assembled, and that group should design an exercise for the rest of the audience. The team may need to leave the room to design the exercise. Alternatively, the larger group can be given a break while the team creates its design.

For Non-Business Settings. No special modifications are needed for non-business settings.

For Schools or Homes. The trainer or teacher should lead the children in the design of the new exercise, eliciting suggestions and comments from them. With young children, the trainer should have a new exercise in mind before eliciting any feedback.

Other Options

As noted earlier, trainers should feel free to experiment with the way they conduct all Design Challenge exercises.

Data Collection

The trainer may wish to use or modify Form A.3 in the Appendix of this book (p. 261).

FOLLOW-UP

Discussion Questions

1) What was the goal of this exercise? Did we reach that goal? Why or why not?
2) How could this exercise be improved?
3) What did this exercise teach us, if anything?
4) How can we relate the outcome of this exercise to the outcomes of the previous exercises in this chapter?
5) Does diverse training have value in the creative process? Have your views on this issue changed at all since we began this series of exercises?

Debriefing

The trainer should comment on the exercise in the context of the previous sections in this chapter.

Long-Term Follow-Up

This exercise does not require a long-term follow-up. As usual, however, if there has been a dramatic result, it should be preserved and posted.

COMMENTS

As usual in the Design Challenges, trainers need to ensure: (a) that everyone gets a chance to participate, (b) that the exercise is fun and upbeat, and (c) that time limits are respected. If several exercises are to be conducted, the trainer will need to schedule breaks.

EXERCISE: WORKPLACE CHALLENGE

BASICS

Objective

To extend the lessons of the previous exercises in this chapter to specific organizational settings.

Brief Description

Participants are asked to design an application, procedure, or policy (a) that is based on principles, methods, or outcomes from previous exercises in this chapter and (b) that has specific benefits for their particular workplaces.

Required Materials and Supplies

Writing materials.

Optional Materials and Supplies

Large, blank sheets of paper (without lines) should be available to encourage people to make diagrams or drawings. Word processors may be helpful in some settings.

Time Requirement

Minimum: 20 minutes. Maximum: 1 hour.

PROCEDURE

Basic Procedure

Trainer (modify as appropriate): "Our next step is to try to extend what we've learned to our particular organizational setting. If broadening has value in the creativity process, how can we improve our workplace to take advantage of that fact? How could we provide training to direct the creative process toward specific goals? What policies or procedures might we change? How might we improve the work environment? How might we change or improve our training procedures? What other changes might we make? What outcomes—positive and negative—might we expect to result from such changes?

"Let's take ten minutes to sketch out our ideas. In the spirit of the exercises we've just completed, try to 'stay loose.' Don't be overly concerned just yet about the practicality of your suggestions. Don't think too much about budget. Just think, 'How might my organization be improved to take advantage of the fact that diverse training spurs creativity?' After ten minutes have passed, I'll ask some of you to share your ideas with the group, and we'll discuss them together. Any questions?"

Customizing the Procedure

For Small Groups. In a small group, everyone should be given an opportunity to present his or her ideas. The trainer should emphasize the value of every idea, no matter how impractical. *After* all of the ideas have been presented, the group can begin the task of assessing their feasibility and value.

For Large Groups. In a large group, everyone can sketch out ideas on paper, but the trainer will be able to call on only a few people to present them to the group.

For Non-Business Settings. No special modifications are needed for non-business settings.

For Schools or Homes. Children may need close supervision by the trainer or teacher.

Other Options

Participants might be allowed to work together in teams (although see the caveats in Chapter 8 of this volume). Where an audience includes members of different organizations, the trainer should make sure that each organization is given some consideration.

In settings in which feasibility, dollar-value, and other practical matters are of special concern, the exercise can be expanded to include a discussion of such issues. Remember, however, that when you pass judgment on creative thinking, you tend to discourage it.

Data Collection

Trainers may wish to use or modify Form A.1 in the Appendix of this volume (p. 261).

FOLLOW-UP

Discussion Questions

1) Does your organization provide diverse training to its employees?
2) Is the training optimal to maximize creativity? How might it be optimized?
3) How could very narrow training stifle the creative process?

4) Providing diverse training can have multiple benefits for an organization. What benefits can you think of?

Debriefing

Trainer (modify as appropriate): "We've seen that training can be used both to enhance creativity and to direct it toward specific ends, and we've also tried to envision how we might use training regimes in our own organization to enhance and direct creativity."

Long-Term Follow-Up

Workplace Challenges should be followed up whenever possible. The trainer should encourage participants to complete and return Form A.2 (or some equivalent), which can be found in the Appendix of this volume (p. 261), thirty days after the completion of training. See the Follow-Up section in Section 3.6 for further remarks.

COMMENTS

Some organizations spend vast sums on training; others consider it a luxury. The fact that you're in the process of conducting a training session on creativity suggests that your organization is in the former category. If not, your participants may complain that the present exercise is an exercise in futility—a pipedream, if you will. If so, encourage pipedreaming, and remind your trainees that that's what this particular training session is all about. Some of those pipedreams may prove to be the first steps toward constructive changes in the organization.

BROADENING:
GENERAL DEBRIEFING

Training is expensive, no doubt about it. And ignorance is even more expensive, as our local school boards keep reminding us. In the business world, it has long been recognized that there's a return on your investment when you invest in training, but the emphasis has usually been on gains in competence. In the exercises we just completed, we explored another benefit of training: an increase in creativity.

Training will have its greatest impact on creativity when it expands the margins of people's knowledge. If you've already taken fourteen courses on computer networking, that fifteenth course may make you marginally more competent, but it won't make you more creative. A course in artificial intelligence, however, may get you to look at networking with an entirely new pair of eyes. You might end up boosting the IQ level of your network by thirty points, or perhaps you'll bring new networking techniques to AI.

To boost creativity, training should be as diverse as possible within the domain of interest, defined broadly. Moreover, the greatest leaps will come when *other* domains—once thought to be irrelevant—are brought to bear on the original domain. How can you know in advance where these leaps will come from? Should you learn more about materials science? Biotechnology? The World Wide Web? Nanotechnology? It's impossible to say. But when in doubt, *find it out*. Where creativity is concerned, diverse training is never wasted. The knowledge you acquire today will be available to "resurge" when the appropriate problem arises. Knowledge is never wasted.

Here are the major points we explored in the exercises in this section:

- Difficult problems are easy to solve when people have had the right training, as we saw in the "News" exercise.

- In "The Broader the Better," we considered the fact that when people think about multiple domains of knowledge, they can usually generate more ideas than when they think about a single domain of knowledge.

CHAPTER 7

"SURROUNDING" GAMES: WHAT SHOULD I PUT ON MY DESK?

SURROUNDING:
ORIENTATION

As we've seen, one way to get many behaviors competing with each other is through extinction. The other way is by surrounding yourself with diverse stimuli, both social and physical. If red and green were illuminated at the same time on a traffic light, you'd be inclined to stop and go and the same time, and, of course, you'd also feel confusion—the feeling you experience when behaviors are in competition. If you were together for the first time with your boss and your child, you'd also feel confused and frustrated at times; you'd be inclined to say things to your child that would feel awkward in front of your boss, and you'd be inclined to say things to your boss that would feel awkward in front of your child.

We can put this simple effect of "multiple controlling stimuli" to good use. We can promote creativity by deliberately surrounding ourselves with multiple stimuli, and we can keep our thoughts fresh by changing those stimuli frequently.

We'll explore these ideas further in the following exercises. In "The Toys-as-Tools Game," we'll look at the effect that physical stimuli can have on our creativity, and in "The Audience Game," we'll see if the presence of other people can affect our creative thinking. In the Design and Workplaces Challenges that follow, we'll extend and apply this ideas.

EXERCISE: "THE TOYS-AS-TOOLS GAME"

BASICS

Objective

To demonstrate that a rich assortment of current stimuli helps spur the creative process.

Brief Description

Participants are asked to invent new children's toys, given either no toys to examine or many toys to examine.

Materials and Supplies

You'll need an assortment of small children's toys, as diverse as possible. Be sure you have at least a dozen; the more, the better. You'll also need a table in front of the room on which to display the toys. None of the toys should be on display when you start the exercise. You might want to keep them all in a box just behind the table. The display of toys should be obscured by a partition, so that only about half of the trainees can see the toys (see diagram below). You'll need a blackboard or flipchart on which to collect your results. Participants will need writing materials; you may want to duplicate copies of Form 7.2.1 for this purpose.

The exercise can also be conducted without toys using Form 7.2.2 (see Other Options, below).

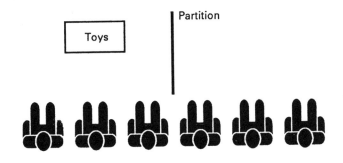

Time Requirement

Minimum: 30 minutes. Maximum: 1 hour.

PROCEDURE

Basic Procedure

Trainer (modify as needed): "In this exercise, called 'The Toys-as-Tools Game,' we're all going to become inventors. Please get your writing materials ready, and I'll set up some special materials in front of the room. Not all of you will be able to see them, however."

Set up the partition, table, and toys, as indicated above. Then continue: "You now have the pleasant task of inventing some new children's toys. Please describe as many new toys as you can in the next fifteen minutes."

After fifteen minutes have passed, ask people how many ideas they've generated, as follows: "Please stop writing. Some of you have done your creating relying on what you remember about children's toys. The rest of you have had the benefit of being able to see an assortment of children's toys. Let's see how the two groups did."

Get a tally of the number of ideas people had in the two groups by asking for a show of hands. On the blackboard, complete a chart like the one shown in Figure 7.2.1. Unless you have the same number of people in each group, you'll need to compute the percentages for each category, as shown in the figure. The toys group should be able to generate far more ideas than the no-toys group.

Discuss the results with your participants.

Customizing the Procedure

For Small Groups. In a small group, you may be able to arrange the seats so that you have the same number of people in the toys and no-toys conditions. That will save you the trouble of computing percentages.

For Large Groups. In a very large group, a rough tally may be all you'll need to make your point.

For Non-Business Settings. No special modifications are needed for non-business settings.

For Schools or Homes. This exercise won't work very well with active users of toys, so it's not meant for young children.

Other Options

If you like, you can conduct the exercise without real toys. Simply distribute Form 7.2.1 to half the group and Form 7.2.2 to the other half. After fifteen minutes have elapsed, do the tally as described above.

Data Collection

The most important data are the aggregate data. If you want to preserve them, you'll need to copy them from the blackboard.

FOLLOW-UP

Discussion Questions

1) Did the presence of toys help people to invent new ones? Why or why not?
2) How do diverse stimuli accelerate the creative process?
3) What should you put on your desk to promote creativity?

Debriefing

Trainer (modify as needed): "Although we've used children's toys in this exercise, it should be easy to extrapolate to the real world. Our surroundings are often dull and unchanging. Enriching and changing our surroundings will make us more creative.

"The toys demonstration is a simple one, but it makes an important point. When we need to generate new ideas, we tend to rely entirely on our memories to get us started. That's heroic, but there's no need to be so hard on ourselves. There's no substitute for a rich environment."

Long-Term Follow-Up

No special follow-up is needed for this exercise. You may want to refer back to this exercise, however, if you follow-up on the Workplace Challenge. And, as usual, if you get some spectacular results, try to preserve and display them.

COMMENTS

In some training rooms, you may find it difficult to prevent half of your audience from viewing the toys. In that case you may want to use the paper-and-pencil option, or get "creative" in the way you seat your trainees!

Figure 7.2.1. *Ask for a show of hands to complete a tally of ideas as follows:*

	TOYS GROUP no.	TOYS GROUP %	NO-TOYS GROUP no.	NO-TOYS GROUP %
>15				
10-14				
5-9				
<5				

Participant's Notes and Evaluation
Exercise: "The Toys-as-Tools Game"

Please invent as many new toys as you can in the allotted time:

1.	11.
2.	12.
3.	13.
4.	14.
5.	15.
6.	16.
7.	17.
8.	18.
9.	19.
10.	20.

To share data or comments with the author, fax this form to 619-436-4490.

*From **Creativity Games for Trainers**, by Dr. Robert Epstein. E-mail address: repstein@rohan.sdsu.edu.*

"The Toys-as-Tools Game" (Continued)

Participant's name and contact information (optional):

_____
_____
_____
_____

Organization:
_____
_____

Position:
_____
_____

Date:
_____
_____

Trainer:
_____
_____

Value of the exercise:
_____

LOW   ☐   ☐   ☐   ☐   ☐   HIGH
_____

Suggestions for improving the exercise:
_____
_____
_____
_____
_____

Participant's Notes and Evaluation
Exercise: "The Toys-as-Tools Game"

Please invent as many new toys as you can in the allotted time. Here are some toys that already exist:

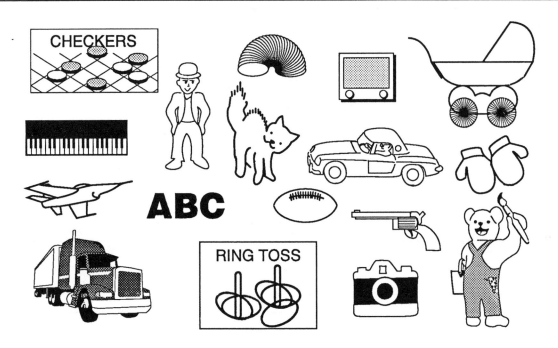

1.

2.

3.

4.

5.

6.

7.

8.

9.

10.

11.

12.

13.

14.

15.

16.

17.

18.

19.

20.

*To share data or comments with the
author, fax this form to 619-436-4490.*

*From **Creativity Games for Trainers**, by Dr. Robert
Epstein. E-mail address: repstein@rohan.sdsu.edu.*

"The Toys-as-Tools Game" *(Continued)*

Participant's name and contact information (optional):

_____

_____

_____

_____

Organization:

_____

_____

Position:

_____

_____

Date:

_____

_____

Trainer:

_____

_____

Value of the exercise:

LOW ☐   ☐   ☐   ☐   ☐   HIGH

Suggestions for improving the exercise:

_____

_____

_____

_____

_____

EXERCISE: "THE AUDIENCE GAME"

BASICS

Objective

To show that the presence of other people can enhance creativity.

Brief Description

Some volunteers perform a naming task while facing the audience and others while facing away from the audience.

Materials and Supplies

You'll need six chairs that you can move around in front of the room, as well as writing materials for your volunteers. Forms 7.3.1 and 7.3.2 can be used, if you like.

Time Requirement

Minimum: 15 minutes. Maximum: 30 minutes.

PROCEDURE

Basic Procedure

The trainer should select six volunteers and seat three of them so that they face the audience and the other three facing away from the audience. If your space allows, place the latter three people so that they can't see each other, either. If necessary, you can do the exercise with fewer volunteers (see customizing options, below). Give writing materials to all of the volunteers. Forms 7.3.1 and 7.3.2 can be employed.

Trainer: "As you can see, I've got six volunteers here. Three of them can see the audience, and three cannot. I've asked the latter three to keep their eyes away from the audience and away from each other at all times. Our volunteers are going to help us discover the effects that social stimuli—in other words, the effects that you, the audience—can have on creativity.

"Volunteers, are you ready? Here are your instructions: You've been made Secretary of Labor, and the President wants to you to help her inspire confidence in the economy. Your assignment: to invent has many new *job titles* as you can. These can be new titles for jobs that people already have, or they can be titles for jobs that don't actually exist. The President wants to use these job titles in an upcoming speech. She wants to meet with you in *ten minutes,* so you'll have to work fast.

"One more thing: Whenever you add a job title to your list, raise your hand high for a moment so that we can see your progress. Any questions?"

Have people start writing, and have a timekeeper notify you when ten minutes have elapsed. For added drama, have a scorekeeper keep a simple tally on a blackboard or flipchart: The tally should show the number of times people raise their hands in each of the two groups—Audience and No-Audience.

When the time is up, inform the audience of the total count in each of the two groups, elicit some examples of job titles from each group, and lead a discussion about the results. The Audience group will normally produce more job titles than the No-Audience group.

Customizing the Procedure

For Small Groups. This exercise is not well suited for groups of fewer than twenty people, but it's worth a try. (Experiment! Be creative!) If you have only ten people in your group, you certainly don't want six volunteers sitting up front. That would leave an audience of only four people—too little stimulation to produce the predicted outcome. You might try using just four or even two volunteers. The problem with using a smaller number of volunteers is that you increase the risk that an "outlying point" will skew your results. If the volunteer who's facing away from the group just happens to write job titles for the Personnel Department, you're in trouble.

For Large Groups. If your room is large enough, you might try the following seating arrangement for your volunteers:

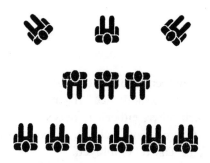

For Non-Business Settings. In a non-business setting, you might want to give your volunteers a different task. Almost any task that would be facilitated by social stimuli is worth trying. Consider: (1) "Hairdos and haircuts have been given many interesting names over the years, such as 'crew cut,' 'afro,' 'shag,' and 'flat top.' You job is to create new names for hair styles. They may be new names for existing hair styles, or names for hair styles that don't actually exist." (2) "Items of clothing have been given many interesting names over the years, such as 'tank top,' 'dickey,' 'baggies,' and 'bell bottoms.' Your job is to create new names for items of clothing. They may be new names for existing items of clothing, or names for items of clothing that don't actually exist."

For Schools or Homes. Ideally, the group should be relatively large (say, over twenty), and the task should be appropriate to the group.

Other Options

You might try increasing the work period to fifteen minutes. Longer time periods should accentuate the difference between the groups.

You might also consider using a different task. See the "For Non-Business Settings" section above for some suggestions.

Data Collection

Forms 7.3.1 and 7.3.2 can be used to help you collect data.

FOLLOW-UP

Discussion Questions

1) Did the two groups (Audience and No-Audience) produce different results? What were the results, and why did they differ?

2) Did the individuals in the two groups behave in a noticeably different way during the task? How so?

3) Social stimuli would normally improve performance on a task like this. Why?

4) Can you think of a task in which social stimuli would lower performance?

5) In a group or team situation in which everyone can participate, social stimuli are often inhibiting. Why would that normally not be the case in the task we just completed?

Debriefing

Trainer (modify as needed): "People are rich sources of stimuli. As such, they can and should be utilized to boost creativity, especially when people are trying to generate ideas that have to do with other people. In other words, to enhance our creativity, we should surround ourselves with interesting and diverse physical and social stimuli—and that includes people. On the other hand, people can and do often have a profoundly inhibiting effect on creativity, for the simple reason that people often show signs—subtle and not-so-subtle—that they disapprove of our new ideas. It's the disapproval that we received while being socialized that has brutally suppressed the creative potential of most people. In the current exercise, the audience was passive. They didn't know what the volunteers were writing and hence had no reason or opportunity to criticize. So the volunteers facing the audience were able to benefit from the presence of the audience without having to face the disapproval of the audience."

Long-Term Follow-Up

No long-term follow-up is needed. Interesting results should be preserved, as usual.

COMMENTS

The predicted effect may not appear if the audience is too small. Even in that case, however, you should be able to see a difference in the way the individuals in the two groups behave: In the Audience group, the volunteers should frequently scan the audience, very obviously "looking for ideas," almost as if they were relying on ESP to help them. In the No-Audience group, the volunteers will appear to stare off into space, as if they are straining to *imagine* other people. As a starting point for creativity, real stimuli are usually more helpful than imagined stimuli. They're certainly more vivid.

Chapter 8 explores in more detail the advantages and disadvantages of actually working in groups.

Participant's Notes and Evaluation
Exercise: "The Audience Game"
Audience Group

Given the trainer's instructions, please list as many examples as possible in the allotted time:

1.

2.

3.

4.

5.

6.

7.

8.

9.

10.

11.

12.

13.

14.

15.

16.

17.

18.

19.

20.

"The Audience Game" (Continued)

Participant's name and contact information (optional):

_____

_____

_____

_____

Organization:

_____

_____

Position:

_____

_____

Date:

_____

_____

Trainer:

_____

_____

Value of the exercise:

LOW   ☐   ☐   ☐   ☐   ☐   HIGH

Suggestions for improving the exercise:

_____

_____

_____

_____

_____

*From **Creativity Games for Trainers**, by Dr. Robert Epstein. E-mail address: repstein@rohan.sdsu.edu.*

Participant's Notes and Evaluation
Exercise: "The Audience Game"
No-Audience Group

Given the trainer's instructions, please list as many examples as possible in the allotted time:

1.	11.
2.	12.
3.	13.
4.	14.
5.	15.
6.	16.
7.	17.
8.	18.
9.	19.
10.	20.

To share data or comments with the author, fax this form to 619-436-4490.

*From **Creativity Games for Trainers**, by Dr. Robert Epstein. E-mail address: repstein@rohan.sdsu.edu.*

"The Audience Game" (Continued)

Participant's name and contact information (optional):

_____

_____

_____

_____

Organization:

_____

_____

Position:

_____

_____

Date:

_____

_____

Trainer:

_____

_____

Value of the exercise:

LOW   ☐   ☐   ☐   ☐   ☐   HIGH

Suggestions for improving the exercise:

_____

_____

_____

_____

_____

_____

To share data or comments with the author, fax this form to 619-436-4490.

*From **Creativity Games for Trainers**, by Dr. Robert Epstein. E-mail address: repstein@rohan.sdsu.edu.*

EXERCISE:
DESIGN CHALLENGE

BASICS

Objective

To further demonstrate the role that surrounding plays in the creative process by having the participants themselves design an exercise that makes this point.

Brief Description

Participants are asked to spend a few minutes designing another exercise along the lines of the previous exercises in this chapter. They then carry out the new exercise. They may require the trainer to participate.

Materials and Supplies

They may use (a) any of the materials and supplies from the previous exercises in this chapter and (b) any additional materials, objects, or supplies that are present in the room.

Time Requirement

Minimum: 30 minutes. Maximum: 90 minutes.

PROCEDURE

Basic Procedure

Trainer: "In the exercises we've just completed, we've seen that creativity can be enhanced when we surround ourselves with interesting stimuli—both social and physical. Your task now is to design a new exercise that will further demonstrate what we have learned. You'll have ten minutes in which to design this new task. Here are some guidelines: (a) you can make use of any of the objects and materials that we've used in previous exercises; (b) you can make use of any other objects or materials in this room; (c) you can assign people to different roles and send people out of the room, as necessary; (d) you can use me as one of the participants in this new exercise. After the ten-minute design period is over, you'll have an additional ten minutes in which to conduct the exercise. After that, a representative from your group will lead us all in a short debriefing to evaluate the outcome of the new exercise and to see whether your goals have been met."

Customizing the Procedure

For Small Groups. Small groups can be broken up into teams of approximately five people each. Each team should design its own exercise. If time allows, each team should be allowed to conduct the exercise it has designed, using the trainer and the other teams as participants.

For Large Groups. In a large auditorium where time is limited, a single team should be assembled, and that group should design an exercise for the rest of the audience. The team may need to leave the room to design the exercise. Alternatively, the larger group can be given a break while the team creates its design.

For Non-Business Settings. No special modifications are needed for the non-business setting.

For Schools or Homes. The trainer or teacher should lead the children in the design of the new exercise, eliciting suggestions and comments from them. With young children, the trainer should have a new exercise in mind before eliciting any feedback.

Other Options

As noted earlier, trainers should feel free to experiment with the way they conduct all "Design Challenge" exercises. See Section 3.5 for further details.

Data Collection

The trainer may wish to use or modify Form A.3 in the Appendix of this book (p. 261).

FOLLOW-UP

Discussion Questions

1) What was the goal of this exercise? Did we reach that goal? Why or why not?
2) How could this exercise be improved?
3) What did this exercise teach us, if anything?
4) How can we relate the outcome of this exercise to the outcomes of the previous exercises in this chapter?
5) Can diverse and interesting stimuli in our environment help boost our creativity? Have your views on this issue changed at all since we began this series of exercises?

Debriefing

The trainer should review any interesting results and praise the participants for their design efforts.

Long-Term Follow-Up

This exercise does not require a long-term follow-up. As always, however, if there has been a dramatic result, it should be preserved and posted.

COMMENTS

As always, trainers need to ensure: (a) that everyone gets a chance to participate, (b) that the exercise is fun and upbeat, and (c) that time limits are respected. If several exercises are to be conducted, the trainer will need to schedule breaks.

EXERCISE:
WORKPLACE CHALLENGE

BASICS

Objective

To extend the lessons of the previous exercises in this chapter to specific organizational settings.

Brief Description

Participants are asked to design an application, procedure, or policy (a) that is based on principles, methods, or outcomes from previous exercises in this chapter and (b) that has specific benefits for their particular workplaces.

Required Materials and Supplies

Writing materials.

Optional Materials and Supplies

Large, blank sheets of paper (without lines) should be available to encourage people to make diagrams or drawings. Word processors may be helpful in some settings.

Time Requirement

Minimum: 20 minutes. Maximum: 1 hour.

PROCEDURE

Basic Procedure

Trainer (modify as appropriate): "Our next step is to try to extend what we've learned to our particular organizational setting. If the stimuli that surround us—both social and physical stimuli—have the potential to enhance our creativity, how can we improve our workplace to take advantage of that fact? What policies or procedures might we change? How might we improve the work environment? How might we change or improve our training procedures?

What other changes might we make? What outcomes—positive and negative—might we expect to result from such changes?

"Let's take ten minutes to sketch out our ideas. As usual, try to 'stay loose.' Don't be overly concerned just yet about the practicality of your suggestions. Don't think too much about budget. Just think, 'How might my organization be improved to take advantage of the fact that diverse physical and social stimuli help spur creativity?' After ten minutes have passed, I'll ask some of you to share your ideas with the group, and we'll discuss them together. Any questions?"

Customizing the Procedure

For Small Groups. In a small group, everyone should be given an opportunity to present his or her ideas. The trainer should emphasize the value of every idea, no matter how impractical. *After* all of the ideas have been presented, the group can begin the task of assessing their feasibility and value.

For Large Groups. In a large group, everyone can sketch out ideas on paper, but the trainer will be able to call on only a few people to present them to the group.

For Non-Business Settings. No special modifications are needed for non-business settings.

For Schools or Homes. Children may need close supervision by the trainer or teacher.

Other Options

You may want to have participants work together in small groups (although see the caveats in Chapter 8 of this volume). Where an audience includes members of different organizations, the trainer should make sure that each organization is given some consideration.

Data Collection

Trainers may wish to use or modify Form A.1 in the Appendix of this volume (p. 261).

FOLLOW-UP

Discussion Questions

1) How can the surroundings in your organization be improved to stimulate creativity?
2) Does you plan include provisions for changing the surroundings periodically? Why is this important?
3) Does your present work environment help or hurt creativity? How so?
4) Could changes of the sort you've suggested actually be implemented by your organization? Why or why not?

5) If you anticipate implementation problems, can you think of creative ways to solve those problems?

Debriefing

Point out some of the more interesting proposals, and praise everyone for rising to the Workplace Challenge. Almost any effort should be encouraged.

Long-Term Follow-Up

Workplace Challenges should, whenever possible, be followed up. The trainer should encourage participants to complete and return Form A.2 (or some equivalent) in the Appendix of this volume (p. 261) thirty days after the completion of training. Did participants try to implement any of their ideas? If so, what were the results? If not, why not? See Section 3.6 for further details.

COMMENTS

As always, you should allow people considerable leeway in how they choose to meet this challenge. Throughout this workshop, the trainer serves an important function by encouraging creativity in almost any form. Moreover, participants should always be encouraged to capture their good ideas, whether or not those ideas are relevant to the present assignment.

SURROUNDING: GENERAL DEBRIEFING

Have you ever been to an artist's studio or to the private study of a fiction writer? Typically, you're bombarded by interesting and diverse stimuli: weird sketches and photographs, plastic models, scraps of paper taped to the walls, and outright junk that should have been thrown away years ago. Environments that are diverse and complex help keep repertoires of behavior in competition, and that keeps new ideas flowing. There's a downside, of course. Such environments are disturbing and confusing, because that's how we feel when behaviors are competing in our nervous system. A noisy environment is also distracting, and that might prevent us from capturing our thoughts. What's the solution?

To help us capture our new ideas (Chapter 3), we need to find the best times and places to pay attention to them. But to keep us thinking in new ways, we also need to put ourselves—at least occasionally—into rich environments. If all you have on your desk are pictures of your children and stacks of paperwork, your thinking will probably be narrow. Imagine that same desk with a couple of playing cards on it, face up, and some clippings from this week's *National Enquirer*. Would you find your thoughts wandering at times? I don't mean to suggest that you use these particular stimuli, of course. You should choose stimuli that suit your needs. But diverse stimuli make for diverse thinking.

What's more, it's important that you alter the stimuli frequently. Move the desks and chairs around. Switch offices. Switch floors. Change where you sit in the cafeteria. Take a different route home. Change work partners. Change clubs. Bring people together who normally would never meet.

With ever-changing stimuli, your ideas will stay fresh.

CHAPTER 8

TEAM CREATIVITY:
IS IT BETTER
TO BE ALONE?

TEAMS: ORIENTATION

Organizations typically employ teams to generate new ideas. Speaking of ideas, is that one we should buy? Are teams good for creativity?

That groups hurt creativity in certain ways has long been known. A small number of aggressive people typically dominate any group; the creative contributions of the majority of the participants are never heard. Status, prestige, and management level will lead some people to defer to others; the fresh ideas of young employees are never expressed. Personal relationships, alliances, conflicts, and struggles over resources—that domain we politely call "politics"—create a poor atmosphere for free expression.

Experts have developed many techniques for reducing the impact of such factors. Brainstorming, the seven hats technique, and so on, are all fundamentally "role-playing" techniques: Some rules are established that will, one hopes, get people behaving in special ways for the duration of the meeting. "We won't pass judgment on new ideas" or "Jane will be the risk-taker" or "For the next hour, we'll all be at the same level of management" are typical rules that people try to follow.

But no set of rules will change people's memories. The conflicts and pecking orders and personalities are still there, and everyone knows it. People won't give away a pencil unless the politics are right. How about a million dollar idea?

In one critically important respect, the team is the worst possible place to ask someone to be creative. Why? Because a team is the most likely place to find signs of disapproval. Since age six, it's been disapproval that has kept most people from showing the slightest hint of creativity. Is a roomful of colleagues the right place to ask someone to abandon a lifetime of inhibition?

The people we typically call "creative"—artists, writers, composers, and so on—are notorious for locking themselves in attics, running away to secluded beaches, or scaring people away with withering scowls. Could Beethoven have composed a symphony while sitting in a room full of marketing professionals?

New ideas arise in individual brains only. No exceptions. Creativity is strictly an individual phenomenon. The generative process is, necessarily, a lonely one. And the presence of other people—all of whom come equipped with eyebrows that might be raised slightly at any moment—is inhibiting.

Then why all the hype about teams as hotbeds of creativity?

Properly managed—with whichever role-playing technique you choose—a team can aid creativity in two ways: First, in a team each individual is surrounded by other people, each of whom can add to or comment on whatever the individual thinks or says. In other words, the team *surrounds* each individual with numerous social stimuli (see Chapter 7). Multiple stimuli will get multiple repertoires of behavior competing, and that, of course, is the starting point for creativity. In a team of ten people, that process is, in effect, multiplied ten times, because it's occurring simultaneously with ten different people. Sounds good, except for all the inhibiting effects of those same people.

Second, a team can serve the legitimate function of *editing* or *modifying* new ideas, especially when those ideas are meant to be applied to a larger population. Teams represent populations far better than individuals do.

So we've got three factors to consider: inhibition (bad), surrounding (good), and editing (good). How can we make this work so that teams will help the creative process more than they hurt it?

In the first exercise in this section, we'll explore a technique called "shifting" as a tool for putting teams to good use. Since creativity is an individual process, perhaps we'll get more and better ideas out of our team if we allow the participants to shift in and out of the team strategically. In the second exercise, we'll let a team function as a "quality editor" for new ideas, and we'll see whether the team is a better editor than each of a number of individuals. Finally, the Design and Workplace Challenges will give people an opportunity to further explore and apply these ideas.

EXERCISE:
"THE SHIFTING GAME"

BASICS

Objective

To demonstrate some of the ways that teams both help and hurt creativity.

Brief Description

Some participants work as a team to solve a problem, while other participants shift in and out of a team. The outcome of the two strategies is compared.

Materials and Supplies

Two blackboards or flipcharts would be helpful. Participants will also need pads and pencils. If your space allows, set up ten chairs in front of the room, in two groups of five. The chairs can be placed around two small tables, or they can face inward in two small circles. A stopwatch or large timer clock would be helpful.

Time Requirement

Minimum: 40 minutes. Maximum: 90 minutes.

PROCEDURE

Basic Procedure

Trainer (modify as necessary): "Let's try a group exercise called 'The Shifting Game.' I'll need two teams, five people in each, to get us started."

Select the members of each team and send the teams out of the room. Select a timekeeper to help you with the timing.

Trainer: "Next, we'll need a task for the teams to work on. A naming task would be ideal, something like: 'McDonald's is going to introduce the first fast-food non-fat hamburger. Think of as many names as you can for this new hamburger.' Suggestions for a task?"

Have the group help you pick a target task. Naming tasks tend to work well.

Bring both teams back into the room, seat them in the chairs in front of the room, and instruct them as follows: "In just a moment, I'm going to give you a job to do—a job that was designed by your colleagues here in the audience—but I need each team to tackle the job a little differently. Team One, you'll have ten minutes in which to complete your task, and it's important that you work together as a team at all times. *It's important that your members not work as individuals at any time.* If you wish to elect a leader to impose some structure on your proceedings, that's up to you. Team Two, your members will need to work on the task *as individuals*—without any group interaction—for five minutes before you work together as a team. I'll signal you when five minutes have passed, at which point you should *shift* from the individual mode to the team mode. Any questions?

"Okay, here is the task. Remember that your job is to generate *as many answers as possible* to the problem we're posing."

Tell the teams the task, and start the clock running.

When five minutes have passed, signal Team Two to shift to team mode. When ten minutes have passed, have a representative from each team list on the blackboard or flipchart the suggestions that have been generated by each team. Note any differences in the two lists, and lead a discussion about the advantages and disadvantages of "shifting."

Customizing the Procedure

For Small Groups. In a small group, everyone can participate in this exercise. Simply divide the group into teams of four or five people. Have half of the teams work on the task without the group-shift, and have the other teams do the shift. The task can be selected by an "executive committee," or you can simply impose the task.

For Large Groups. In a large group, two teams of five should work well. If your space won't accommodate ten chairs in front of the room, you can have the teams work on opposite sides of the room, or even outside the room.

For Non-Business Settings. This exercise can work well in non-business settings. The key is to select a task that's appropriate to the participants.

For Schools or Homes. This game is a bit too demanding for young children. Ironically, it is only *after* we have become well socialized that we can work together in unsupervised groups. While children are still young enough to act freely on their creative impulses, they'll tend to perform poorly in games of this sort.

Other Options

If time allows, or if you're ready to experiment, try more than one shift—for example, four periods alternating between individual creativity and team creativity.

Data Collection

Form 8.2.1 can be used to help collect data.

FOLLOW-UP

Discussion Questions

1) Which team produced more ideas, Team One (non-shifting) or Team Two (shifting)?
2) In general, a shifting team should produce more and better ideas than a non-shifting one. Why?
3) How does a team foster creativity among its members?
4) How does a team hinder creativity among its members?

Debriefing

Trainer: "Creativity is an individual phenomenon, not a group phenomenon. All new ideas spring from individuals—from individual brains. There are no exceptions to this rule. Teams can both help and hurt the process by which an individual creates. They help because they are powerful sources of 'multiple controlling stimuli' (see Chapter 7 on 'Surrounding'). In a team, every individual gets stimulation from every word and movement of the other participants. That can certainly foster an individual's creativity, and since everyone is having on impact on everyone else, the effect is multiplied. If you suggest 'Healthburger' as a name for the new McDonald's hamburger, someone near you is bound to say, 'No, it's got to have the *mac* prefix,' to which you'll immediately respond, *'MacHealthburger.'* The stimulation you're getting will keep multiple repertoires of behavior competing.

"Teams are also superb *editors* of ideas, a concept we'll explore in our next exercise.

"But teams also tend to hinder the creative process, because they are inhibiting. As school children, we learned to hide our creative sides, and most of us still find it difficult to share our new ideas with other people—especially the raw stuff that we haven't had time to edit yet. We could never have gotten or kept a job if we hadn't been well socialized. As socialized creatures, most us will shut down creatively in a group.

"What about 'brainstorming,' 'the seven hats technique,' and other role-playing techniques for fostering creativity in a team? All of the role-playing techniques try to reduce the likelihood of ridicule or punishment; they'll reduce inhibitions to the extent that they are successful in that regard. But our long history of socialization cannot be undone by mere role playing, and a variety of research shows unequivocally that even the most subtle forms of negative feedback—like the raised eyebrow—can have devastating effects. Even while role playing, people know very well who the hostile players are, and they can easily detect signs of disapproval. Some participants will remain silent, and many, if not most, new ideas, will never get a hearing. People might be willing to behave more humanely for a few minutes in a role-playing exercise, but they don't leave their memories behind.

"Consequently, teams need to be used in a special way to maximize creativity: The surrounding and editing functions have value; the inhibiting function does not. The solution is *shifting*—allowing people to go off on their own to work on the problem before returning to the team. *Anonymous suggestions systems* (Section 4.4) can be combined with shifting to produce even more creative output."

Long-Term Follow-Up

At a thirty-day follow-up, you may want to ask participants whether they have tried any shifting and what the result was. You can also follow-up through the Workplace Challenge (Section 8.5).

COMMENTS

Team Two (shifting) should end up with a longer list of ideas than Team One does, but there are exceptions to every rule. If you get the "wrong" result, the first thing to explore is *how* Team One carried out its task. You may find that the participants did spend a few minutes working on their own, in spite of your instructions. If your training area is noisy, you may also find that the members of the Team Two were distracted when working individually. Usually, the non-shifting team (One) will waste time getting organized before digging in. In the shifting team (Two), participants start working immediately, because they're working on their own; they don't have organizational issues to wrestle with. Then, typically, they pool their ideas, eliminate duplicates, and add a few more to the list. By the time the members of Team Two meet, they have a lot of material with which to work.

Participant's Notes and Evaluation
Exercise: "The Shifting Game"

Task to be completed by each team:

Team One (Non-Shifting) Ideas	Team Two (Shifting) Ideas

Did the two teams perform differently? Yes ☐ No ☐ Why or why not?

To share data or comments with the author, fax this form to 619-436-4490.

*From **Creativity Games for Trainers**, by Dr. Robert Epstein. E-mail address: repstein@rohan.sdsu.edu.*

"The Shifting Game" (Continued)

Participant's name and contact information (optional):

_____

_____

_____

_____

Organization:

_____

_____

Position:

_____

_____

Date:

_____

_____

Trainer:

_____

_____

Value of the exercise:

LOW   ☐   ☐   ☐   ☐   ☐   HIGH

Suggestions for improving the exercise:

_____

_____

_____

_____

_____

_____

EXERCISE: "THE TEAM AS QUALITY EDITOR"

BASICS

Objective

To show the special value that a team has in editing and selecting ideas.

Brief Description

The group as a whole generates a list of twenty new cola names. Then five people work together to select the best three names, in order of preference. While the team is deliberating, the remaining members of the audience work individually to select their own three choices. Finally, the individual lists are compared to the group-generated list.

Materials and Supplies

Everyone will need writing materials, and you'll also need a place for a group of five people to hold a brief private meeting. They can meet outside the training room. You'll also need a blackboard or flipchart in front of the room.

Time Requirement

Minimum: 15 minutes. Maximum: 30 minutes.

PROCEDURE

Basic Procedure

Trainer (modify as needed): "In this brief exercise, we'll look at one of the truly unique and important functions that the team plays in the creative process. As you'll see, this function has little to do with the *generation* of new ideas and more to do with the *selection* of new ideas. To start, I'll ask all of you to help me compile of list of names for a new cola that's to be released in a few months. It's intended as the ultimate competitor to Coke and Pepsi, and its producers intend to control a third of the cola market within a year. They believe that the name alone will account for sixty percent of their sales, so the right name is worth several billion dollars. We've been asked to recommend three names. The final selection will be based on extensive marketing surveys. What do you suggest as a name for the new cola?"

List the suggestions on the blackboard or flipchart until you have between twenty and twenty-five names. Then continue: "We now have considerably more names than we can recommend, so we'll need to narrow down the list. We're going to do that in two different ways. First, may I have five volunteers to serve on a special editors team?"

Assemble the team, and continue: "I'm going to ask our editors to leave the room for a few minutes. While outside, they need to work together to select the top three names, in order of preference. Any questions from our editors?"

Send them out of the room, and continue: "While our editors are working, I'd like everyone here—working individually—to make their own choices. Please write your top three selections, in order of preference, from most to least preferred. No collaborating, please."

After a few minutes—and before you bring the editors back into the room—ask three people, chosen at random, for their top choices. Write these on the board (see Figure 8.3.1). Then bring the editors back into the room, and ask them to report their own top three choices. Write these on the board as well (Figure 8.3.1).

Have the volunteers return to their seats, and continue: "We now have four lists on the board, one of them developed by a team and the others by individuals. Let's decide which list we're going to submit to the makers of the new cola. We'll do this in two different ways. First, let's try simple comparison votes. To make the process fair, I'm going to ask our editors to refrain from voting."

By a show of hands, have the audience show their preference for List 1 (Team) versus List 2 (Individual), List 1 versus List 3, and List 1 versus List 4 (Figure 8.3.1). Next, get a rank-ordering of the four lists by having people vote for one list only among each of the four (Figure 8.3.1). Exclude the editors from each vote.

Trainer: "Normally, a team-selected list of new ideas is superior to an individually selected list of new ideas, at least in one important respect. It is likely to be preferred by the population of people from which the team is drawn." (See additional discussion below.)

Customizing the Procedure

For Small Groups. As long as you have more than ten people in your group, the procedure given above should suffice. With a smaller group of trainees, you'll need to assemble a smaller team of editors. Just be sure than the team of editors is substantially less than half the size of the group of trainees.

For Large Groups. With a very large group, you may run into the same problem that survey professionals have. When assembling your team of editors, you may unwittingly select a sample that does not represent the group. Volunteers "self-select," and people who do so tend to be especially bold. Use your best judgment to select representative editors for this exercise; if necessary, use random numbers or other sampling methods to help you stay objective. You can also assemble a larger team of editors. (For other shady statistical maneuvers, consult your local survey professional.)

For Non-Business Settings. No special modifications are necessary for non-business settings, other than cosmetic changes in the instructions. Rather than having people name a cola, you may want to choose an open-ended task that suits the setting.

For Schools or Homes. The major point of this exercise—that teams are good editors of creative output—will be of little interest to most young people.

Other Options

There's nothing sacred here about the cola problem. Choose a problem that suits your needs. Just be sure that it's an open-ended task. A naming task is ideal simply because it yields brief, one-word answers that can easily be compared. Long answers are difficult to compare, and they don't fit easily on a blackboard.

If you want to get elaborate, you can use other methods, such as preference scales, to have the audience score the lists. If your editors team is representative of your audience, almost any method you use should show the superiority of the editors' list.

Data Collection

Only the blackboard has the key data for this exercise. You may want to preserve a copy of the material, either for data-sharing purposes or for future reference.

FOLLOW-UP

Discussion Questions

1) Teams can both help and hurt the creative process. In what ways?
2) Teams serve an essential role as editors of creative output. What can a team accomplish that an individual cannot?
3) Was the editors' list preferred by the larger group of trainees? Why or why not?
4) Are teams used in your organization to produce new ideas? Are teams used optimally for this purpose? If not, what improvements can you suggest?

Debriefing

Trainer (modify as needed): "Creativity is an individual process, in the sense that ideas always arise in individuals. After all, generative mechanisms exist in a single brain, and, as we all know too well, groups don't have a brain. But it's important that the raw creative output from individuals be subjected to the scrutiny of teams, and it is in that sense that teams play an essential role in the creativity of an organization. In an organization, new ideas have value only if they serve many people; individuals are usually poor judges of the value that their new ideas may have for the larger community."

Long-Term Follow-Up

This exercise can best be followed up through the Workplace Challenge in this chapter.

COMMENTS

As noted above, if your team of editors isn't representative of your trainees, their list may not be preferred over the lists obtained from individuals. If the worst happens, analyze the result with the group, and learn from it. If you pick five people who are all dressed the same or who are sitting next to each other, expect less than ideal results.

Figure 8.3.1. *Blackboard Schematic.*

TEAM	INDIVIDUALS		
LIST 1	LIST 2	LIST 3	LIST 4
1.	1.	1.	1.
2.	2.	2.	2.
3.	3.	3.	3.

PAIRED COMPARISONS

LIST 1 _____ LIST 2 _____ WINNER: _____

LIST 1 _____ LIST 3 _____ WINNER: _____

LIST 1 _____ LIST 4 _____ WINNER: _____

RANK ORDER

VOTE: LIST 1 ____ 2 ____ 3 ____ 4 ____

RANK: LIST 1 ____ 2 ____ 3 ____ 4 ____

EXERCISE:
DESIGN CHALLENGE

BASICS

Objective

To further explore the effect that teams have on creativity by having the participants themselves design a relevant exercise.

Brief Description

Participants are asked to spend a few minutes designing another exercise along the lines of the previous exercises in this chapter. They then carry out the new exercise. They may require the trainer to participate.

Materials and Supplies

They may use (a) any of the materials and supplies from the previous exercises in this chapter and (b) any additional materials, objects, or supplies that are present in the room.

Time Requirement

Minimum: 30 minutes. Maximum: 90 minutes.

PROCEDURE

Basic Procedure

Trainer: "In the exercises we've just completed, we've looked at the possible role that teams can play in enhancing creativity. Your task now is to design a new exercise to further explore the effects that teams can have on the creative process—either positive or negative effects. You'll have ten minutes in which to design this new task. Here are some guidelines: (a) you can make use of any of the objects and materials that we've used in previous exercises; (b) you can make use of any other objects or materials in this room; (c) you can assign people to different roles and send people out of the room, as necessary; (d) you can use me as one of the participants in this new exercise. After the ten-minute design period is over, you'll have an additional ten minutes in which to conduct the exercise. After that, a representative from your group will lead us all in a short debriefing to evaluate the outcome of the new exercise and to see whether your goals have been met."

Customizing the Procedure

For Small Groups. Small groups can be broken up into teams of approximately five people each. Each team should design its own exercise. If time allows, each team should be allowed to conduct the exercise it has designed, using the trainer and the other teams as participants.

For Large Groups. In a large auditorium where time is limited, a single team should be assembled, and that group should design an exercise for the rest of the audience. The team may need to leave the room to design the exercise. Alternatively, the larger group can be given a break while the team creates its design.

For Non-Business Settings. No special modifications are needed for the non-business setting.

For Schools or Homes. The trainer or teacher should lead the children in the design of the new exercise, eliciting suggestions and comments from them. With young children, the trainer should have a new exercise in mind before eliciting any feedback.

Other Options

As noted earlier, trainers should feel free to experiment with the way they conduct all Design Challenge exercises. See Section 3.5 for further comments.

Data Collection

The trainer may wish to use or modify Form A.3 in the Appendix of this book (p. 261).

FOLLOW-UP

Discussion Questions

1)   What was the goal of this exercise? Did we reach that goal? Why or why not?
2)   How could this exercise be improved?
3)   What did this exercise teach us, if anything?
4)   How can we relate the outcome of this exercise to the outcomes of the previous exercises in this chapter?
5)   How can teams help and hurt the creative process? Have your views on this issue changed at all since we began this series of exercises?

Debriefing

The debriefing should be conducted by a representative from the design team or teams. The trainer should participate only as needed.

Long-Term Follow-Up

This exercise does not require a long-term follow-up. As usual, however, if there has been a dramatic result—a surprising or significant example of creativity, for example—that result should be preserved and posted.

COMMENTS

As always, you'll need to ensure: (a) that everyone gets a chance to participate, (b) that the exercise is fun and upbeat, and (c) that time limits are respected. If several exercises are to be conducted, you'll need to schedule breaks.

EXERCISE:
WORKPLACE CHALLENGE

BASICS

Objective

To extend the lessons of the previous exercises in this chapter to specific organizational settings.

Brief Description

Participants are asked to design an application, procedure, or policy (a) that is based on principles, methods, or outcomes from previous exercises in this chapter and (b) that has specific benefits for their particular workplaces.

Required Materials and Supplies

Writing materials.

Optional Materials and Supplies

Large, blank sheets of paper (without lines) should be available to encourage people to make diagrams or drawings. Word processors may be helpful in some settings.

Time Requirement

Minimum: 20 minutes. Maximum: 1 hour.

PROCEDURE

Basic Procedure

Trainer (modify as appropriate): "Our next step is to try to extend what we've learned to our particular organizational setting. If teams need to be employed in special ways to enhance creativity, how can we put that knowledge to use? What policies or procedures might we change? How might we improve the work environment? How might we change or improve our training procedures? What other changes might we make? What outcomes—positive and negative—might we expect to result from such changes?

"Let's take ten minutes to sketch out our ideas. In the spirit of this workshop, try to 'stay loose.' Don't be overly concerned just yet about the practicality of your suggestions. Don't think too much about budget. Just think, 'How might my organization be improved to take advantage of the fact that teams need to be used in special ways in order to enhance creativity in the organization?' After ten minutes have passed, I'll ask some of you to share your ideas with the group, and we'll discuss them together. Any questions?"

Customizing the Procedure

For Small Groups. In a small group, everyone should be given an opportunity to present his or her ideas. The trainer should emphasize the value of every idea, no matter how impractical. *After* all of the ideas have been presented, the group can begin the task of assessing their feasibility and value.

For Large Groups. In a large group, everyone can sketch out ideas on paper, but the trainer will be able to call on only a few people to present them to the group.

For Non-Business Settings. No special modifications are needed for non-business settings.

For Schools or Homes. Children may need close supervision by the trainer or teacher.

Other Options

You might want to have people to work together in teams, but you should probably insist that people shift in and out of the teams. If the audience includes members of different organizations, you should make sure that each organization is given some consideration.

Data Collection

Trainers may wish to modify Form A.1 in the Appendix of this volume (p. 261).

FOLLOW-UP

Discussion Questions

1)   Does your organization currently use teams in an optimal way to enhance creativity? Please explain.

2)   How, currently, do team practices help or hurt creativity in your organization?

3)   What changes could improve the way teams are used to affect creativity in your organization?

Debriefing

The trainer should review some of the more interesting proposals and note how they apply what the group has learned about the role that teams play in creativity.

Long-Term Follow-Up

Workplace Challenges should, whenever possible, be followed up. The trainer should encourage participants to complete and return Form A.2 (or some equivalent) in the Appendix of this volume (p. 261) thirty days after the completion of training. See Section 3.6 for further remarks.

COMMENTS

Some participants may have little interest in how teams are utilized in their organization. They should still be encouraged to complete the exercise. Challenge stimulates the creative process; they'll probably come up with *something* interesting to say, even if it's a little off task. If all they could think of was a way to improve service in the company cafeteria, encourage them to *capture* that idea (see Chapter 3).

TEAMS:
GENERAL DEBRIEFING

When it comes to creativity, the team is a mixed blessing. To all but the aggressive few, a team is inhibiting, even intimidating. Yet teams also provide multiple social stimuli, which have the potential to stimulate creativity by putting multiple repertoires of behavior in play.
In this portion of our training, we explored the following issues:

- Creativity is an individual process, not a group process. New ideas occur in individual brains.

- As we saw in the "Shifting" exercise, we can get more ideas out of a team if we allow members to shift in and out of the team. Many good ideas will occur to people when they're on their own.

- Role-playing techniques cannot erase people's memories, but they are important in managing group dynamics to encourage at least a reasonable level of participation and free expression.

- Teams serve a unique and valuable function as "quality editors" for new ideas, especially when those ideas are intended for use with a larger population. As we saw in the second exercise, teams are better representatives of a population than individuals are.

CHAPTER 9

KEYS TO CREATING INNOVATIVE PRODUCTS, SERVICES, AND PROCESSES

MANAGING CREATIVITY:
ORIENTATION

At this point, we've taken a long, hard look at the creative process and at some strategies for managing it. In this last section, we'll try some fairly complex exercises, and we'll also address the bottom line, also known as "innovation." The latter term is reserved for a small subset of creative ideas—those that have market value. The training in this volume has focused, deliberately, on creativity, not innovation, for two reasons: First, you can't skip creativity on the way to innovation. Innovative ideas are always drawn from a larger pool of creative ones. Increase the size of the creativity pool, and you get more innovation. Creativity is, in effect, a primary process, and innovation is a secondary process. Second, the tools that we've developed in this book can be applied to *any* problem, including the problem of innovation. In other words, if you've already got plenty of new ideas in your organization, but none of them ever gets to market, you've got a problem that needs a solution. That's the time to start problem solving using the many techniques we've explored. A technology of creativity can be helpful not only in dreaming up new products and services but also in correcting systemic problems in your organization.

Creativity and innovation can be engineered. With appropriate changes in policies and procedures, and, when applicable, an appropriate allocation of resources, the creative output of an organization can be increased many times over. How, specifically, one achieves this depends on the particular characteristics of the organization. That's not a cop-out, it's just the simple truth. As any engineer can tell you, when you're building a bridge, principles get you only five percent of the way. Most of your energies are devoted to a careful study of the terrain. The principles are essential to the whole enterprise, of course, but mainly because they provide a framework for studying the terrain.

You should have some real fun with the three exercises that follow. In the first, "The Keys to Creativity," volunteers will try to retrieve a set of keys that are out of reach. The solution is tricky, and the supervisor is demanding—just like in the real world. In Part Two of the exercise, many irrelevant stimuli are added to the problem to make it even harder—again, just like reality. As you should expect by now, people will solve the problem anyway, as long as you give them enough time. The exercise provides a powerful demonstration of the value of waiting, as well as a moving example of the creative process in action.

In "Building Bridges to Creativity," small teams get to play with colorful foam "tub" blocks. With such great toys, the exercise should be successful even if it doesn't teach anything. The chances are good, however, that the exercise will show how instructions can affect the creativity of teams.

In "The Ultimate Design Challenge," participants are asked to turn their organization on its head within ten days—increasing the creative and innovative output by at least a factor of ten. The exercise can be easily modified or expanded to focus on innovation per se (see "Other Options," p. 252).

After the Final Debriefing (Section 9.5), I'll slip in one final exercise, called "The Waiting Game." It's simple and persuasive, like the "Daydream" exercise, and it's a great way to end a workshop.

EXERCISE: "THE KEYS TO CREATIVITY"

BASICS

Objective

To show various creative processes at work in a series of complex problems.

Brief Description

Using various tools, volunteers try to retrieve a set of keys that are out of reach.

Materials and Supplies

You'll need a footstool, a key ring (1-inch inner diameter) with about 5 keys on it, masking tape, a standard mop or broom, and an assortment of children's toys.

Time Requirement

Minimum: 45 minutes. Maximum: 90 minutes.

PROCEDURE

Basic Procedure

Part One. Be sure the equipment for the game is out of sight. Then select two volunteers and send them out of the room. Tell them that you'll be calling them back into the room one at a time to solve a simple problem. Appoint a timekeeper.

Trainer (modify as needed): "And now, the keys to creativity [trainer pulls out the ring of keys]. Our volunteers will have to retrieve these keys using various tools that I provide. As you will see, we're going to make them work hard to get these keys; we're going to use what we've learned in this workshop to get the generative apparatus running in high gear. What's more, we're going to see how good we've become at understanding and predicting creative behavior. To some extent, we're all now experts on creativity. Let's see if we can put our expertise to work."

Next, set up the materials while explaining what you're doing to the group. Place the footstool in front of the room, and put the ring of keys on the stool. *Important:* Place the ring so that it protrudes upward toward the ceiling (see diagram, below); from the vantage point of the volunteer, it should look like the letter O. Next, place a four-foot length of masking tape on the floor about six feet away from the stool. The masking tape should be perpendicular to the front wall of the room (see diagram). Finally, place the mop or broom next to the masking-tape line, on the side opposite from the stool.

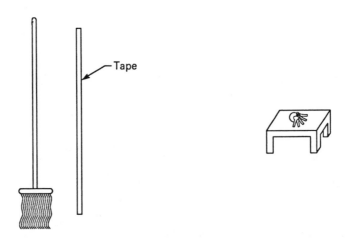

Trainer: "Our volunteers' task will be to retrieve the ring of keys without crossing this line [point] and without letting the keys touch the ground. Our first volunteer will be able to use this mop [point]. As you will see, there are many ways to solve this problem, but we're looking for one particular solution.

"Let's see if we can predict what our first volunteer will do in this situation. We have a large key ring and a mop with a long handle on it. What's the first thing to try?

"Most people will extend the handle toward the beckoning key ring and try to spear it [demonstrate]. It looks like it will fit, but the ring is just a bit too small. So this behavior will fail, which should give us some *extinction effects:* frustration, resurgence, and so on. We should also see signs of new behavior.

"There's one very simple solution to this problem. Some people get it right away, and some people get it shortly after they've failed to spear the key ring with the broom handle. While trying to spear the keys, people move the keys slightly, or they even jar the stool. Aha! They've now got a new stimulus that makes them think about moving the stool, at which point they use the mop head to draw the stool toward them, and they retrieve the keys [demonstrate this solution, and then restore the stool and keys to their original positions].

"But we're not going to let them off so easy. Here's the solution we're looking for. [Unscrew the mop head or broom head and use the tapered end of the handle to hook the key ring.] This may seem difficult, but so is the real world. What's more, people *always* get this solution—*given enough time*."

Replace the mop head, set up the keys again properly (so that the ring looks like an upright O when you're behind the line), place the mop on the floor beside the line, and call in the first volunteer.

Instructions to the volunteer: "Please stand here, behind this line [point]. Your task is to retrieve that set of keys [point]. You must not cross the line; you may not ask anyone to help you; and you must not let the keys touch the floor. You may use this mop [point] to help you. Any questions?"

The timekeeper should time the performance until the easy solution (pulling the stool) is achieved. That time should be recorded.

If the keys fall to the floor, you'll need to position them again. Once the easy solution has been achieved, congratulate the volunteer, restore the stool and keys to their original positions, and continue as follows: "Great job, but a memo has just come down from a Senior VP complaining about the costs involved in moving mountains. So you'll need to solve the problem another way, this time without moving the stool. Please continue."

The solution should emerge in the next five-to-ten minutes. Along the way, you may need to reassure the volunteer that the problem can actually be solved. The statement "You can do it!" may be all you'll need. Be patient, and, if necessary, tell jokes. Generative processes take time, and frustration is a sign that the processes are working. If you give the answer away, you'll be sending out two unfortunate messages: (1) I don't practice what I preach, and (2) I have no confidence in our volunteer.

If time is short, and the solution seems to be hours away, here's a suggestion: Send the first volunteer out of the room again "to take a break." Bring in the second volunteer and continue with Part Two of the exercise. Then set up the materials for Part One, bring in the first volunteer again, and give that volunteer another chance. (I've only had to do this once, and the result was well worth the effort. I gave a telephone company executive several chances throughout the day to solve the problem, while the workshop continued on track. She got a standing ovation when she finally solved the problem, and she said she felt like she had just won the lottery.)

When the solution has been reached, ask for observations from the audience, and then proceed to Part Two.

Part Two. Before you bring in the second volunteer, restore the key ring, mop, and stool to their original positions, and then place an assortment of children's toys in the vicinity of the mop (on the mop side of the line, not the stool side). I usually use a plastic baseball bat, a set of dominoes, a tennis ball, a plastic ring, and some foam blocks. The more the merrier, but you're probably better off with toys that cannot easily be used to solve the problem (see the Comments section, below). Tell the group: "Our second volunteer will have the same problem to solve, but with a real-world twist. I've added a number of irrelevant objects to the playing field. What effect should this have on our volunteer's performance?"

Bring in the volunteer, and continue: "Please stand here, behind this line [point]. Your task is to retrieve that set of keys [point]. You must not cross the line; you may not ask anyone to help you; and you must not let the keys touch the floor. You may use these objects [point] to help you. Any questions?"

Have the timekeeper keep track of how long it takes the volunteer to achieve the easy solution (pulling the stool). When that has been achieved, continue as you did in Part One: Set up the problem again, and tell the volunteer that the stool cannot be moved.

If the volunteer stumbles onto a solution you hadn't anticipated, offer your congratulations, "requisition" the offending toy, and have the volunteer start again.

Your task in this exercise is to be tough, pushing creativity to its limits until the desired solution is reached. This may sound burdensome, but it's actually great fun for everyone.

Customizing the Procedure

For Small Groups. No special modifications are needed.

For Large Groups. In a large auditorium, you may want to use a video camera and projection equipment to give the audience a clearer view of what the volunteers are doing.

For Non-Business Settings. In non-business settings, simply substitute the appropriate language for the business language used in this exercise.

For Schools or Homes. For young children, you'll need to simplify both the problem and the instructions to suit the group.

Other Options

This exercise can be scaled up or down in many ways. If time is very short, skip Part Two. If time is not quite so limited, skip Part One. If you want to explore the effects of using other distractors, repeat the exercise with a third volunteer.

As always, you can also change the instructions to suit your training needs.

Data Collection

You'll need a camcorder to collect data in this exercise. Paper and pencil don't do justice to it.

FOLLOW-UP

Discussion Questions

1) In what ways were the two performances predictable? In what ways were they surprising?

2) How did the previous experience of the volunteers play a role in their performances?

3) Did you see signs of frustration at any point? What other extinction effects did you observe?

4) Note the times it took for the two volunteers to reach the easy solution (pulling the stool). Did the irrelevant toys slow down the second volunteer at all? Why or why not?

5) How were the conditions in this exercise like those of the real world? How were they unlike those of the real world?

6) This exercise shows that "multiple controlling stimuli" spur creativity, but that they also delay the appearance of a solution. How does it show that?

7) How does this exercise demonstrate the importance of waiting?

Debriefing

Trainer (modify as needed): "You now have the 'keys to creativity'—or at least our volunteers do! Here are some of them: (1) *Waiting* is important when we're looking for new ideas. Generative processes take time. (2) *Multiple controlling stimuli* lead to new ideas, but they can also delay the appearance of solutions to particular problems. In the real world, it's hard to tell the good stimuli from the bad. (3) *Frustration* is a bothersome but essential part of the creative process. (4) The creative process is *orderly,* and that's a fact that we can use to our advantage. (5) *Everyone* has enormous creative potential."

Long-Term Follow-Up

No specific follow-up is needed.

COMMENTS

"Keys to Creativity" is probably the most memorable exercise in this volume. Done well, it's full of drama and fun, and it's a powerful demonstration of the orderliness of the creative process. I've used this exercise in the laboratory, in classrooms, and in business settings for over five years, and I've never seen it fail. Often members of the audience will stand and cheer for the volunteers.

In a way, the exercise can't fail, as long as the trainer stays calm. When I first began doing the exercise with managers, invariably the first volunteer would look at someone in the audience and say, "Excuse me. Could you retrieve those keys for me?" I simply replied, "Sorry, but a memo from the CEO just announced that the members of our audience are too busy to help you." When someone found a way to use a badminton racket to solve the problem (I'm not telling how!), I retrieved the racket and said, "Sorry, OSHA has just prohibited the use of badminton rackets in our work environment." Make life difficult for your volunteers, and keep reminding them that the real world does the same. Your trainees will forgive you.

On the other hand, there are a couple of errors you should avoid: Make sure that the key ring cannot be speared with the round end of the mop handle. Similarly, make sure that it's easy to spear the key ring with the tapered end (once the head is removed). The stiff bristles on broom heads can sometimes be used to snag the key ring; you're better off with soft dust mops or dusters. Also, be certain that the footstool is far enough behind the line so that people can't lean over to reach the keys and that it's close enough to allow people to reach the keys with the end of the mop handle. Finally, choose your toys to achieve the end you have in mind. I tend to use toys that lead to dead ends, leaving only the easy solution (pulling the stool) and the hard solution (unscrewing the mop head), but that's only because I'm usually pressed for time. For more fun, use more toys.

One last comment: Every time I've done this exercise, I've been surprised. The volunteers have always managed to do something I've never seen before. Watch carefully; I suspect you'll have the same experience.

EXERCISE: "BUILDING BRIDGES TO CREATIVITY"

BASICS

Objective

To show the importance of open-ended instructions in a team activity.

Brief Description

Two teams build bridges using foam blocks, having first been given slightly different instructions.

Materials and Supplies

You'll need a bucket of fifty lightweight foam blocks, sold commercially under the name "Tub Blocks." You'll also need two sheets of white legal-size paper, a marker, and a ruler. Two small tables, spaced well apart, should be set up in front of the room.

The Tub Blocks, all of which are one-inch thick, come in a variety of shapes. You'll need to create two identical sets of blocks, one for each team. In each set, I suggest you include the following blocks:

(2)	6-inch by 1.5-inch rectangles
(4)	3.5-inch by 1.5-inch rectangles
(4)	3-inch by 1.5-inch rectangles
(1)	3-inch square
(2)	triangles
(2)	half-circles
(2)	circles

It isn't critical that you use exactly these blocks or that you use this particular brand. Before you begin the exercise, however, be sure that you practice building bridges with whatever materials you've decided to employ.

On the sheets of paper, mark two parallel lines, ten inches apart, as shown at the top of the following page. The space between the lines will be the "river" in the exercise.

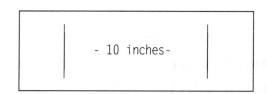

Time Requirement

Minimum: 20 minutes. Maximum: 40 minutes.

PROCEDURE

Basic Procedure

Before displaying the materials, appoint two teams, three people in each, and send them out of the room. Appoint a timekeeper.

Trainer (to audience): "Challenge is important to the creative process, and one of the ways we create challenge is through the instructions we give. Sometimes very subtle differences in instructions can make a huge difference in creativity. In this exercise, 'Building Bridges to Creativity,' I'll give slightly different instructions to each of our two teams, and we'll see how, or if, performance is affected. When we bring our teams back into the room, I'll give each of them their instructions in writing.

"The first team will read, 'Your task is to use the provided building blocks to span a river, marked by two parallel lines on the sheet of paper on the table. In your final structure, no blocks may touch the space between the two lines. You have a maximum of ten minutes in which to complete this task.'

"The second team will read, 'Your task is to use the provided building blocks to build the widest possible bridge that you can. At a minimum, it must span a river, marked by two parallel lines on the sheet of paper on the table. In your final structure, no blocks may touch the space between the two lines. You have a maximum of ten minutes in which to complete this task.'

"The instructions to the two teams are, for all practical purposes, identical. In neither team are we specifying a *maximum* span. But in the second team, we're *emphasizing* the fact that the problem is open-ended and that we attach *value* to a highly efficient use of the limited resources we've provided.

"The question is: Which team will build the bridge with the widest span?"

Place the blocks and "rivers" at each table. Then bring the teams back into the room, station them at their respective tables, and give them their written instructions (Figure 9.3.1). Have the timekeeper start the ten-minute timer running. Using this format, you probably won't be able to take questions from the teams. As they proceed, you can encourage them, and you can also let them review their written instructions.

When the teams have completed their tasks, or when the maximum time has expired, measure the span of each bridge, and then lead a discussion about the effect of open-ended instructions on creative performance.

Customizing the Procedure

For Small Groups. With enough foam blocks and rivers, everyone in the room can have some fun. Simply divide the group into a number of teams. Give half of the teams the Team 1 Instructions and the other half the Team 2 Instructions (Figure 9.3.1). This way, you can compute an *average* span for each type of instruction, which gives you a more valid (and more certain!) outcome.

For Large Groups. In a large auditorium, you might consider using two video cameras to project the two construction projects onto screens. To heighten the drama, you can also set up a partition between the two tables.

For Non-Business Settings. No special modifications are needed.

For Schools or Homes. With the particular blocks I've listed above, the problem is too difficult for many children. One solution is to reduce the width of the river to five inches.

Other Options

This exercise can be done with individuals instead of teams. The main advantage of using teams is to make more hands available to place the blocks and hold the structure steady during the construction process.

Data Collection

You may want to keep track of the spans and designs that your various teams produce. If any team achieves a span over sixteen inches (with the blocks I've designated), please let me know!

FOLLOW-UP

Discussion Questions

1) Did the two teams perform differently? How so?
2) How do open-ended tasks, open-ended instructions, and open-ended questions differ from conventional tasks, instructions, and questions?
3) How do open-ended tasks improve creative performance? How is resurgence involved?

Debriefing

Trainer: "Typically, Team 2 outperforms Team 1 in this task, even though the instructions we gave to Team 1 do not actually specify any performance maximums. The problem is that for most people, performance maximums are always *implied,* even when they're not stated. To get the generativity wheels rolling at high speed, it's important to make tasks explicitly open-ended. This gets people into the controlled failure mode; that gets the extinction processes going; and that get's repertoires competing. The result: more effort, and more creativity."

Long-Term Follow-Up

At a thirty-day follow-up, inquire whether participants have experimented with using open-ended instructions.

COMMENTS

There many ways to use the designated blocks to build bridges with spans greater than ten inches. Even sixteen inches is possible. Although it won't get you the largest possible span, one principle that makes bridge-building easy is *counterbalancing.* Here's an example:

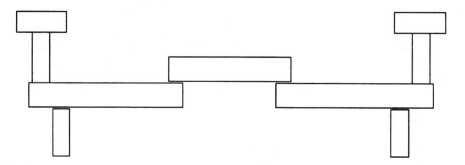

One caveat: If you share this design with your trainees, you may not get much more from them. When people "know the answer" to a problem, creativity takes a nose dive. As I've indicated a number of times in this text, failure is bothersome and frustrating, but it's also extremely helpful in the creative process.

Figure 9.3.1. *Instructions for the Two Teams.*

Team 1

Your task is to use the provided building blocks to span a river, marked by two parallel lines on the sheet of paper on the table. In your final structure, no blocks may touch the space between the two lines. You have a maximum of ten minutes in which to complete this task.

Team 2

Your task is to use the provided building blocks to build the *widest possible bridge* that you can. At a minimum, it must span a river, marked by two parallel lines on the sheet of paper on the table. In your final structure, no blocks may touch the space between the two lines. You have a maximum of ten minutes in which to complete this task.

EXERCISE: "THE ULTIMATE DESIGN CHALLENGE"

BASICS

Objective

To spur participants into designing comprehensive organizational changes that will increase creativity and innovation.

Brief Description

Participants shift in and out of small teams with the goal of developing at least ten ways to increase creativity and innovation in their organization by a factor of ten or more within the next ten work days.

Materials and Supplies

At a minimum, you'll need pads and pencils for everyone. If you elect to have representatives present their results to the group, you'll also need a blackboard, a flipchart, or other presentation materials.

Time Requirement

Minimum: 45 minutes. Maximum: 90 minutes.

PROCEDURE

Basic Procedure

Trainer (modify as needed): "And now, our 'Ultimate Design Challenge.' In a moment, I'll present you with a problem, and I'll do so in a particular way—one that shouldn't surprise you at this late stage of our training. First, I'll need you to break up into teams of between four and six people. Make sure that everyone has writing materials."

After organizing your teams, continue as follows: "Here is your challenge. You must develop a minimum of ten methods for increasing creativity and innovation in your organization by a factor of ten or more. In other words, if you usually get about five new ideas a week, you must now get at least fifty new ideas a week. What's more, these methods must be fully implemented and fully effective within the next ten workdays; that means you must achieve this goal in ten days or less. In other words, two weeks from now your organization must be a hotbed of new and exciting ideas, and your new procedures must guarantee that this high level of creative output will continue year-round.

"To complete this task, work as individuals for five minutes, and then shift into your teams. If you want to shift out and in again, that's up to you. You'll have a total of twenty minutes to complete this task, after which I'll ask representatives of various teams to present their plans to all of us.

"Note that this problem is open-ended and difficult—a true ultimate challenge. I've asked for *at least* ten methods; they must increase creative output by *at least* a factor of ten; and the goal must be achieved in *no more than* ten days. I'm deliberately pushing you to your limits in order to accelerate generative processes. Note also that we'll be using the shifting technique in an attempt to spur more and better ideas.

"Any questions?"

When five minutes have passed, announce that participants should shift into their teams. When twenty minutes have elapsed, call on representatives of the teams to present the plans.

Customizing the Procedure

For Small Groups. In a small group, all of the teams should make presentations. If time allows, have representatives from each team meet in a "summit" to pool their ideas and create a single, comprehensive plan. The summit can be held outside the training room and a discussion held with the remaining trainees. Alternatively, the summit meeting can be held in the training room and the other trainees can be given a break.

For Large Groups. If your auditorium has fixed, theater-style seats, it may be awkward for people to work together in teams. Nevertheless, I suggest that you endure the chaos for this one exercise. You probably won't be able to call on every one of your teams to make a presentation, and a summit may be impractical.

For Non-Business Settings. No special modifications are needed for non-business settings.

For Schools or Homes. Using appropriate language, the basic task can be used with almost any group; however, children will probably need supervision in order to accomplish the task.

Other Options

The design period can be changed to suit your needs. With a longer design period, you'll get more boredom and frustration, but you'll also get more ideas.

If you like, you can add another part to the exercise in which you focus on innovation per se: "How can you get your organization to increase—by a factor of at least ten—the number of products it brings to market?"

Data Collection

Form 9.4.1 can be used to help collect some of the ideas that people generate.

FOLLOW-UP

Discussion Questions

1) Why not ask for exactly ten methods rather than *at least* ten methods?

2) Should supervisors ever ask for a set number of solutions?

3) Asking for a minimum number of ideas still suggests a limit on how many ideas people should produce. What limit is suggested, and why will many people infer that limit?

4) Could the creative output in your organization actually be increased by a factor of ten or more within the next ten days? Why or why not?

5) Were any good ideas generated in this exercise? What proportion of the ideas that were generated could actually be implemented?

6) Was shifting helpful? Why or why not?

7) How might an anonymous suggestion system make this exercise even more successful?

8) How else might this exercise be improved to yield even more good ideas for improving your organization?

Debriefing

Trainer (modify and expand as appropriate): "We had two goals in this exercise: first, to generate some useful ideas for your organization, and second, to put to use some of the knowledge we've gained about the creative process. Did we achieve these goals?

"In the real world, it can take thousands of new ideas to yield one of value. To get a great idea, it helps to have a large pool to choose from. That's what we're after in an exercise like the one we just completed. We're trying to generate that large pool, after which we can be selective. Why not go directly to the good ideas? Because that's not how creativity works. The generative mechanisms that underlie creativity aren't selective, and unless we allow those mechanisms to operate freely, we won't have many new ideas from which to make selections."

Long-Term Follow-Up

If you plan some follow-up activities, this exercise should probably get special attention. Did participants attempt to implement any of the ideas that were generated in this exercise? What were the results? Have participants tried to use the format of this exercise to generate solutions to other problem? What was the outcome?

In order to ask specific questions, you may want to keep copies of the ideas that were generated by your trainees during the exercise, especially the list generated by the "summit" team.

COMMENTS

As long as you can manage the chaotic activity of small groups, you should have few problems with this exercise. You may find that some teams generate fewer that ten methods in the time allotted; more likely, you'll find that most teams will generate exactly ten, or perhaps eleven or twelve. Whenever time is limited, the number of ideas will also be limited, and some people work more slowly than others. So don't be alarmed if there seems to be a shortage of ideas. Ironically, the instructions will probably contribute to the shortage. When you say "give me at least ten," many people will interpret that to mean "ten is all I really want" or "you can get away with giving me ten." You may want to experiment with other forms of the instructions that might produce greater output, such as: "Give me between ten and twenty ideas" or " Give me as many ideas as you possibly can."

Participant's Notes and Evaluation
Exercise: "The Ultimate Design Challenge"

Please list at least ten methods for increasing the creative output in your organization by a factor of ten or more within the next ten workdays:

"The Ultimate Design Challenge" (Continued)

Participant's name and contact information (optional):

_____

_____

_____

_____

Organization:

_____

_____

Position:

_____

_____

Date:

_____

_____

Trainer:

_____

_____

Value of the exercise:

LOW   ☐   ☐   ☐   ☐   ☐   HIGH

Suggestions for improving the exercise:

_____

_____

_____

_____

_____

MANAGING CREATIVITY:
FINAL DEBRIEFING

The three exercises in this section have allowed us to explore some major workshop themes in greater detail:

- In the "Keys to Creativity," we saw, once again, the power of waiting. The longer you wait, the more new ideas you'll see, and even very difficult problems will be solved. The dynamics of generativity take time to play out.

- We also saw that multiple stimuli—in this case, distracting ones—will produce even more ideas, but they will slow down the solution process.

- In "Bridges to Creativity," we explored the idea that open-ended instructions will typically produce more ambitious and more creative performances. This applies to both teams and individuals.

- In our "Ultimate Design Challenge," we gave people free reign to turn their organization into a creativity factory, using the shifting technique, open-ended instructions, and an ultimate challenge.

The exercises and discussions in this text are intended to have several effects: First and foremost, they're intended to teach people about the creative process. I'm a firm believer in teaching people to be independent of their teachers. As the Talmud relates, "Give a man a fish, and he will not be hungry. *Teach* a man to fish, and he will *never* be hungry." Second, the exercises are meant to lower some inhibitions—to get people to express the creative thoughts that are surging through their brains every moment. This also means teaching people, boldly and unequivocally, that *everyone* is creative. Third, the exercises are intended to provide people with practical *strategies* for making their lives or their organizations more creative.

As I noted in the Introduction, this volume is not for the fainthearted. I have deliberately refrained from offering any specific recipes or tools: no decks of cards, no computer programs, no creativity helmets, no organization of consultants. Instead, I have tried to convey general principles that can be applied widely. Because challenge is so important to the creative process, I have also provided a number of structured challenges to encourage people to extend and apply what they've learned—to encourage them to *act* creatively in significant ways. In effect, the exercises are designed to mobilize creative resources that people already have.

Here is an overview of the major themes we've explored in this volume:

- In Chapter 3, in "Capturing a Daydream" and other exercises, we set about to convince people that the mechanisms that underlie creativity are universal. Everyone has enormous creative potential, largely untapped.

- In Chapter 4, through the "Doodles Game" and other exercises, we saw that it is critically important to *capture* new ideas as they occur. The people we usually call "creative" have excellent *capturing skills*, and anyone can master such skills.

- In Chapter 5, through the "Not-for-the-Fainthearted Game" and other exercises, we learned that failure is a powerful way to get many repertoires of behavior competing simultaneously. In other words, failure spurs the creative process. By *challenging* ourselves deliberately, we can boost our creativity substantially.

- In Chapter 6, in "The News You Can Use" and other exercises, we saw that diverse training or *broadening* can both enhance and direct the creative process. For ideas to combine and interact, they must first exist, so appropriate training is essential to creativity.

- In Chapter 7, in the "Toys" game and other exercises, we learned that it is important to *surround* ourselves with diverse and changing stimuli, both social and physical. Multiple stimuli produce multiple repertoires of behavior and hence spur creativity.

- In Chapter 8, through the "Shifting Game" and other exercises, we learned that teams can both help and hurt creativity. Teams are inhibiting, but they also provide multiple stimuli. Creativity is fundamentally an individual process, and teams have special value as *quality editors*.

I hope that, in conducting your workshop on creativity, you have felt free to depart from the material in this text. I hope that you've looked at this volume both critically and creatively. When creativity is at issue, you are likely to have the greatest impact on your trainees if you show that you yourself are willing to take some risks. With risk-taking goes failure, but—as you are teaching in this workshop—failure has great benefits. If you show that you are willing to practice what you preach about creativity, your trainees will applaud you, even when an exercise has an unexpected outcome.

These exercises are part of a long-term research program on the creative process. Much remains to be done, and in that sense this is a work in progress. If you would like to assist in this effort, please share your data and your constructive comments. My fax number is 619-436-4490, and I can be reached by e-mail at repstein@rohan.sdsu.edu. I'll post corrections to this text on my Web page: http://rohan.sdsu.edu/faculty/repstein/index.html.

Robert Epstein

FINAL EXERCISE: "THE WAITING GAME"

What's this? Yet another game, *after* our final debriefing? Yes, here is one more, and it couldn't be simpler—or more persuasive. It's so simple that I'm going to skip the usual introductory material. Here's how it goes:

Trainer (modify as necessary): "You've just spent two-and-a-half days immersing yourselves in the science and technology of creativity. Now you just want to go home. To leave, however, you'll need a key. This last game, 'The Waiting Game,' will get you that precious key to freedom. I want to go home, as well, so I'll play along with you. Here's all you need to do: First, please get into a relaxed position. Now close your eyes, and, with me, observe your thoughts—almost like we did in the daydream exercise a while ago. Stay relaxed, keep your eyes closed, and keep attending to your thoughts while I complete the instructions.

"To get that key to freedom, all you have to do is attend to your thoughts until you detect a new idea. It needn't be the most important idea you've ever had; it only needs to be new. When you observe yourself thinking a thought you've never had before, open your eyes, jot it down, and quietly remain seated until most of us have had a chance to finish. Your new thought may be trivial, or it may change the world. No matter. It symbolizes your new-found childhood, your ability to direct and preserve the creative processes within you.

"Okay, now just keep relaxing... and paying attention... to the new that's within you...."

Options

This simple exercise can be used at the end of the entire training session or at the end of a morning or afternoon session. It can be jazzed up by distributing real keys, printed as mementos of the training session. Each key should contain a blank area where the participants can write their new ideas. There is no need to collect the keys. They're intended as parting reminders of the enormous creative potential each participant has, as well as of the new control and understanding each participant has attained. They're keys to creative freedom.

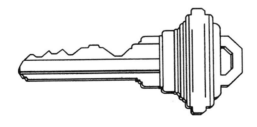

APPENDIX:
ADDITIONAL FORMS

Data Collection Form

Workplace Challenge: _____

How might your workplace be changed to enhance creativity?

To share data or comments with the author, fax this form to 619-436-4490.

*From **Creativity Games for Trainers**, by Dr. Robert Epstein. E-mail address: repstein@rohan.sdsu.edu.*

Data Collection Form: Workplace Challenge (Continued)

Participant's name and contact information (optional):

Organization:

Position:

Date:

Trainer:

Value of the exercise:

LOW   ☐   ☐   ☐   ☐   ☐   HIGH

Suggestions for improving the exercise:

To share data or comments with the author, fax this form to 619-436-4490.

*From **Creativity Games for Trainers**, by Dr. Robert Epstein. E-mail address: repstein@rohan.sdsu.edu.*

264

Follow-Up Form
Workplace Challenge: _____

Date of follow-up:_____ Time elapsed since the training workshop:_____

How, during your training session, had you envisioned changing your organization to enhance creativity? _____

Was it possible to implement any of these changes? Why or why not? _____

If any changes were made, what was the outcome? Has creativity been enhanced? Why or why not? _____

To share data or comments with the
author, fax this form to 619-436-4490.

*From **Creativity Games for Trainers**, by Dr. Robert*
Epstein. E-mail address: repstein@rohan.sdsu.edu.

Follow-Up Form: Workplace Challenge (Continued)

Participant's name and contact information (optional):

_____

_____

_____

_____

Organization:

_____

_____

Position:

_____

_____

Date of training workshop:

_____

_____

Trainer:

_____

_____

Value of the exercise:

LOW   ☐   ☐   ☐   ☐   ☐   HIGH

Suggestions for improving the exercise:

_____

_____

_____

_____

_____

*To share data or comments with the
author, fax this form to 619-436-4490.*

*From **Creativity Games for Trainers**, by Dr. Robert
Epstein. E-mail address: repstein@rohan.sdsu.edu.*

266

Data Collection Form

Design Challenge: _____

Please summarize your design for a new exercise: _____

What was the outcome of this exercise? _____

How could your design be improved? _____

What did you learn from your efforts? _____

To share data or comments with the author, fax this form to 619-436-4490.

*From **Creativity Games for Trainers**, by Dr. Robert Epstein. E-mail address: repstein@rohan.sdsu.edu.*

267

Data Collection Form: Design Challenge (Continued)

Participant's name and contact information (optional):

_____

_____

_____

_____

Organization:

_____

_____

Position:

_____

_____

Date:

_____

_____

Trainer:

_____

_____

Value of the exercise:

LOW ☐ ☐ ☐ ☐ ☐ HIGH

Suggestions for improving the exercise:

_____

_____

_____

_____

_____

_____

To share data or comments with the author, fax this form to 619-436-4490.

*From **Creativity Games for Trainers**, by Dr. Robert Epstein. E-mail address: repstein@rohan.sdsu.edu.*

268

Workshop Feedback Form

Name (optional):_____

Contact information (optional):_____

_____

Trainer:_____ Date:_____

Organization:_____

Location of workshop:_____

Please rate the <u>content</u> of the workshop by circling the appropriate number:

	Definitely Not				Definitely So
The material is interesting.	1	2	3	4	5
It's relevant to my work.	1	2	3	4	5
It has benefited me personally.	1	2	3	4	5
It will benefit my work.	1	2	3	4	5

Please rate the <u>trainer</u> by circling the appropriate number:

	Definitely Not				Definitely So
The trainer was prepared.	1	2	3	4	5
S/he maintained my interest.	1	2	3	4	5
S/he showed mastery of the material.	1	2	3	4	5
S/he encouraged my participation.	1	2	3	4	5
S/he changed my perspective.	1	2	3	4	5

To share data or comments with the author, fax this form to 619-436-4490.

*From **Creativity Games for Trainers**, by Dr. Robert Epstein. E-mail address: repstein@rohan.sdsu.edu.*

Workshop Feedback Form (continued)

Other comments:

Suggestions for improving the workshop:

To share data or comments with the
author, fax this form to 619-436-4490.

From **Creativity Games for Trainers**, *by Dr. Robert*
Epstein. E-mail address: repstein@rohan.sdsu.edu.

Book Feedback Form

Name (optional):_____

Contact information (optional):_____

_____

Trainer:_____   Date:_____

Organization:_____

To help improve future editions of this book, please rate any or all of the following sections by circling the appropriate number:

	Poor				Excellent
Introduction	1	2	3	4	5
1.1. How to Use This Text	1	2	3	4	5
1.2. Materials and Supplies	1	2	3	4	5
2.1. The New Science of Creativity	1	2	3	4	5
2.2. Four Strategies for Enhancing Creativity	1	2	3	4	5
2.3. Dispelling the Myths	1	2	3	4	5
2.4. Games That Teach	1	2	3	4	5
3.1. Creativity: Orientation	1	2	3	4	5
3.2. Capturing a Daydream	1	2	3	4	5
3.3. Selling a Zork	1	2	3	4	5
3.4. The Srtcdjgjklered Game	1	2	3	4	5
3.5. Design Challenge	1	2	3	4	5
3.6. Workplace Challenge	1	2	3	4	5
3.7. Creativity: Debriefing	1	2	3	4	5
4.1. Capturing: Orientation	1	2	3	4	5
4.2. The Random Doodles Game	1	2	3	4	5
4.3. Building a Better Capturing Machine	1	2	3	4	5
4.4. The Anonymous Suggestion Game	1	2	3	4	5
4.5. Design Challenge	1	2	3	4	5
4.6. Workplace Challenge	1	2	3	4	5
4.7. Capturing: Debriefing	1	2	3	4	5
5.1. Challenging: Orientation	1	2	3	4	5
5.2. The Not-for-the-Fainthearted Game	1	2	3	4	5

To share data or comments with the author, fax this form to 619-436-4490.

From **Creativity Games for Trainers**, *by Dr. Robert Epstein. E-mail address: repstein@rohan.sdsu.edu.*

	Poor				Excellent
5.3. The ABCs of Creativity	1	2	3	4	5
5.4. The Ultimate Challenge Game	1	2	3	4	5
5.5. Design Challenge	1	2	3	4	5
5.6. Workplace Challenge	1	2	3	4	5
5.7. Challenging: Debriefing	1	2	3	4	5
6.1. Broadening: Orientation	1	2	3	4	5
6.2. The News-You-Can-Use Game	1	2	3	4	5
6.3. The-Broader-the-Better Game	1	2	3	4	5
6.4. Design Challenge	1	2	3	4	5
6.5. Workplace Challenge	1	2	3	4	5
6.6. Broadening: Debriefing	1	2	3	4	5
7.1. Surrounding: Orientation	1	2	3	4	5
7.2. The Toys-as-Tools Game	1	2	3	4	5
7.3. The Audience Game	1	2	3	4	5
7.4. Design Challenge	1	2	3	4	5
7.5. Workplace Challenge	1	2	3	4	5
7.6. Surrounding: Debriefing	1	2	3	4	5
8.1. Teams: Orientation	1	2	3	4	5
8.2. The Shifting Game	1	2	3	4	5
8.3. The Team as Quality Editor	1	2	3	4	5
8.4. Design Challenge	1	2	3	4	5
8.5. Workplace Challenge	1	2	3	4	5
8.6. Teams: Debriefing	1	2	3	4	5
9.1. Managing Creativity: Orientation	1	2	3	4	5
9.2. The Keys to Creativity	1	2	3	4	5
9.3. Building Bridges to Creativity	1	2	3	4	5
9.4. The Ultimate Design Challenge	1	2	3	4	5
9.5. Managing Creativity: Debriefing	1	2	3	4	5
9.6. The Waiting Game	1	2	3	4	5
Appendix: Additional Forms	1	2	3	4	5
Glossary	1	2	3	4	5
Suggesting Readings	1	2	3	4	5

Comments and suggestions:

To share data or comments with the author, fax this form to 619-436-4490.

*From **Creativity Games for Trainers**, by Dr. Robert Epstein. E-mail address: repstein@rohan.sdsu.edu.*

GLOSSARY

ANONYMOUS SUGGESTION SYSTEM. A suggestion system that promotes capturing by allowing employees to make their suggestions anonymously but then to claim them later. A numbered, two-part form can be used to establish a simple anonymous suggestion system.

BROADENING. Promoting and directing the creative process by seeking or providing diverse training.

CAPTURING. Preserving new ideas as they occur. Capturing can be accomplished with pads and pens, notebooks, napkins, pocket computers, or sticks in the sand. For good capturing, it's essential to identify the best times and places for observing one's novel thoughts. It's also essential to have the right materials on hand.

CHALLENGING. Promoting the creative process by deliberately putting oneself in situations in which one is likely to fail to some extent.

CONTROLLED FAILURE SYSTEM. A system that uses extinction phenomena to promote creativity while keeping employee stress to a minimum.

CREATIVITY. A term used to label novel behavior that has some value to a group or to society. It takes a great deal of novel behavior to yield a small amount of "creativity." In other words, the label is used sparingly, and it's also used differently by different groups.

EXTINCTION. The cessation of reinforcement. Extinction typically has at least five different effects on behavior: (1) the gradual disappearance of the behavior that had been reinforced, (2) the appearance of emotional behavior, (3) an increase in force or magnitude of responding, (4) an increase in the variability of responding, and (5) the resurgence of behaviors that were previously reinforced under similar circumstances in the past.

GENERATIVE BEHAVIOR. The behavior that emerges as a result of a dynamic competition among many behaviors.

GENERATIVITY THEORY. A formal, mathematical theory of creativity and problem solving that suggests that novel behavior is the orderly result of a dynamic competition among many behaviors. Specifically, it suggests that at least four separate processes operate simultaneously on the probabilities of many behaviors and that the result of these simultaneous operations is predictable. The theory utilizes transformation functions in various computer models to simulate or predict creative performances in animals and people.

INNOVATION. A term used to label new products, services, or processes that have monetary value. Only a small portion of the items labeled "creative" are ever labeled "innovative."

MULTIPLE CONTROLLING STIMULI. Diverse stimuli that get many behaviors competing simultaneously.

NOVEL BEHAVIOR. Behavior that is new to the behaving individual, whether or not that behavior has value. Virtually all behavior is novel in some sense.

OPEN-ENDED TASKS. Tasks that have, in theory, an infinite number of solutions, and for which performance maximums are neither stated nor implied.

PUNISHMENT. The presentation of a stimulus that weakens the behavior it follows. Punishment also produces a number of collateral effects: unpleasant emotions, a tendency to counterattack, a tendency to escape, and so on.

REINFORCER. A stimulus that strengthens the behavior it follows.

RESURGENCE. An extinction effect in which behavior that has been successful in the past tends to recur. Resurgence gets many behaviors competing very rapidly and hence spurs the creative process.

SHIFTING. Shifting in and out of a team to maximize creative output.

SURROUNDING. The deliberate use of diverse stimuli—both social and physical—to promote creativity.

ULTIMATE CHALLENGE. An open-ended problem with no feasible solution, used to promote creativity. The ultimate challenge is a technique employed in a controlled failure system.

SUGGESTED READINGS

Adams, James L. (1986). *Conceptual blockbusting: A guide to better ideas, 3rd ed.* Reading, MA: Addison-Wesley.

Amabile, Teresa. (1989). *Growing up creative: Nurturing a lifetime of creativity.* New York: Crown.

Bransford, John. *The ideal problem solver: A guide for improving thinking, learning, and creativity, 2nd ed.* New York: W. H. Freeman.

Campbell, David P. (1985). *Take the road to creativity and get off your dead end.* Greensboro, NC: Center for Creative Leadership.

Carr, Clay. (1994). *The competitive power of constant creativity.* New York: American Management Association.

Dauten, Dale A. (1986). *Taking chances: Lessons in putting passion and creativity into your work life.* New York: Newmarket Press.

de Bono, Edward. (1992). *Serious creativity: Using the power of lateral thinking to create new ideas.* New York: HarperBusiness.

Efron, Robert. (1990). *The decline and fall of hemispheric specialization.* Hillsdale, NJ: Lawrence Erlbaum Associates.

Epstein, R. (1983). Resurgence of previously reinforced behavior during extinction. *Behaviour Analysis Letters*, *3*, 391-397.

Epstein, R. (1985). The spontaneous interconnection of three repertoires. *Psychological Record*, *35*, 131-141.

Epstein, R. (1985). Extinction-induced resurgence: Preliminary investigations and possible applications. *Psychological Record*, *35*, 143-153.

Epstein, R. (1986). Bringing cognition and creativity into the behavioral laboratory. In T. J. Knapp & L. C. Robertson (Eds.), *Approaches to cognition: Contrasts and controversies.* Hillsdale, NJ: Erlbaum, pp. 91-109.

Epstein, R. (1986). Simulation research in the analysis of behavior. In A. Poling & R. W. Fuqua, (Eds.), *Research methods in applied behavior analysis: Issues and advances.* New York: Plenum Press, pp. 127-155.

Epstein, R. (1987). The spontaneous interconnection of four repertoires of behavior in a pigeon. *Journal of Comparative Psychology*, *101*, 197-201.

Epstein, R. (1990). Generativity Theory and creativity. In M. A. Runco & R. S. Albert (Eds.), *Theories of creativity*. Newbury Park, CA: Sage, pp. 116-140.

Epstein, R. (1991). Skinner, creativity, and the problem of spontaneous behavior. *Psychological Science, 6*, 362-370.

Epstein, R. (1992). How to get a great idea. *Reader's Digest*, December, pp. 101-104.

Epstein, R. (1993). Generativity Theory and education. *Educational Technology, 33(10),* 40-45.

Epstein, R. (1994). The creative spark. *Working Mother*, February, pp. 58-59.

Epstein, R. (in press). *Cognition, creativity, and behavior: Selected essays*. New York: Praeger.

Epstein, R., Kirshnit, C. E., Lanza, R. P., & Rubin, L. C. (1984). "Insight" in the pigeon: Antecedents and determinants of an intelligent performance. *Nature, 308*, 61-62.

Epstein, R., & Medalie, S. D. (1983). The spontaneous use of a tool by a pigeon. *Behaviour Analysis Letters, 3*, 241-247.

Epstein, R., & Skinner, B. F. (1981). The spontaneous use of memoranda by pigeons. *Behaviour Analysis Letters, 1*, 241-246.

Foster, R. (1986). *Innovation: The attacker's advantage*. New York: Summit Books.

Gamache, R. Donald. (1989). *The creativity infusion: How managers can start and sustain creativity and innovation*. New York: Harper & Row.

Harman, Willis W. (1984). *Higher creativity: Liberating the unconscious for breakthrough insights*. Los Angeles: J.P. Tarcher.

Hines, Terence. (October 1987). Left brain/right brain mythology and implications for management and training. *Academy of Management Review, 12(4),* 600-606.

Hines, Terence. (1991). The myth of right hemisphere creativity. *Journal of Creative Behavior, 25(3),,* 223-227.

Keil, John M. (1988). *How to zig in a zagging world: Unleashing your hidden creativity*. New York: Wiley.

Klinger, Eric. (1990). *Daydreaming: Using waking fantasy and imagery for self-knowledge and creativity*. Los Angeles: J.P. Tarcher.

Koberg, Don. (1991). *The universal traveler: A soft-systems guide to creativity, problem-solving and the process of reaching goals.* Los Altos, CA: Crisp Publications.

Marra, James L. (1990). *Advertising creativity: Techniques for generating ideas.* Englewood Cliffs, NJ: Prentice-Hall.

Mattimore, Bryan W. (1994). Nine-nine percent inspiration: Tips, tales, and techniques for liberating your business creativity. New York: American Management Association.

Nadler, Gerald, & Hibino, Shozo. (1990). *Breakthrough thinking.* Rocklin, CA: Prima Publishing.

Nelson, Victoria. (1993). *On writer's block: A new approach to creativity.* Boston: Houghton Mifflin.

Shallcross, Doris J. (1981). *Teaching creative behavior: How to teach creativity to children of all ages.* Englewood Cliffs, NJ: Prentice-Hall.

Van Gundy, Arthur B. (1992). *Idea power: Techniques and resources to unleash the creativity in your organization.* New York: American Management Association.

von Hippel, Eric. (1988). *The sources of innovation.* New York: Oxford University Press.

Weisberg, Robert W. (1993). *Creativity: Beyond the myth of genius, 2nd ed.* New York: W. H. Freeman.

Wheelwright, Steven C., & Clark, Kim B. (1992). *Revolutionizing product development: Quantum leaps in speed, efficiency, and quality.* New York: The Free Press.

Wycoff, Joyce. (1991). *Mindmapping: Your personal guide to exploring creativity and problem-solving.* New York: Berkley Books.

ABOUT THE AUTHOR

ROBERT EPSTEIN received his Ph.D. in psychology in 1981 from Harvard University. He has published more than seventy scholarly and scientific articles and has edited two books of writings by the late Professor B. F. Skinner, with whom he worked for five years. He is the developer of Generativity Theory, a scientific theory of creativity, and his research on creativity and problem solving has been reported in *Time* magazine, the *New York Times*, and *Discover*, as well as on national and international radio and television. His scientific writings have appeared in *Science*, *Nature*, the *Proceedings of the National Academy of Sciences*, and he is author of the upcoming book, *Cognition, Creativity, and Behavior: Selected Essays* (Praeger). Dr. Epstein is the founder and Director Emeritus of the Cambridge Center for Behavioral Studies in Massachusetts, and he has been associated with Boston University, the University of Massachusetts at Amherst, the University of California San Diego, and other universities. He has served as Professor of Psychology and Chair of the Department of Psychology at National University in San Diego and was recently appointed the university's first Research Professor. He maintains a laboratory at the Center for Behavioral Epidemiology of the Graduate School of Public Health at San Diego State University. He also directs an artificial intelligence contest offering $100,000 to the designers of the first computer to convince people it's human. Dr. Epstein has done consulting and training for businesses and mental health programs for fifteen years. He has been a commentator for NPR's "Marketplace" and for the Voice of America, and his popular writings have appeared in *Reader's Digest*, *The Washington Post*, *Psychology Today*, *Parenting*, and other magazines and newspapers. He is currently at work on a book called *Totally Fit*^{TM} (Masters Press) with Lori "Ice" Fetrick of television's "American Gladiators."